DATE DUE

MEDITATION
THE ART AND SCIENCE

MEDITATION

THE ART AND SCIENCE

SWAMI VEDA BHARATI

wisdom
tree

© Swami Veda Bharati, 2008

ISBN 978-81-8328-115-7

Published by
Wisdom Tree
4779/23 Ansari Road
Darya Ganj
New Delhi-110002
Ph.: 23247966/67/68

Published by Shobit Arya for Wisdom Tree; *edited by* Manju Gupta; *designed by* Kamal P. Jammual; *typeset at* Marks & Strokes, New Delhi-110002 and *printed at* Print Perfect, New Delhi-110064

CONTENTS

PART ONE

BASICS OF MEDITATION

CHAPTER 1

HISTORY OF MEDITATION

Meditation is 'self-regulation of one's attention in the here and now'. The aim of meditation is to still the mind and take it away from the daily happenings to focus on a pre-selected object. This helps in minimising distraction and focusing on the chosen object. Thus, in short, meditation entails 'mindfulness' and concentration which help the mind from wandering around and focus on a subject of one's choice.

Meditation has three levels: the preparation, the process and the ultimate end. The last two are known as *samadhi*. The last of the *samadhis*, the ultimate end, the ultimate goal, is that in which the mind plays no part because the mind is left behind. It is beyond the mind. Here we must very carefully distinguish between the mind and the self. In the tradition of yoga when we speak of self, we do not refer to the visible personality. We mean *atman*, the self, that is a particular force called the life force, and a particular force called consciousness force, otherwise known in Sanskrit as *jiva*. *Chit* means force of consciousness and is beyond the mind. It controls the mind and directs the mind. It is the seat of awareness and will power. That is the highest *samadhi*, when one truly discovers the non-qualitative self, non-quantative self, and non-conditional self.

Below that is the lower *samadhi* in which the mind plays a part, and that is the one-pointedness of the mind. The word one-pointedness needs to be understood. It does not mean the mind pointed at something. One of the problems in the entire history of Western philosophy and psychology has been that it has not yet, in all the twenty-six centuries of its history, arrived at an agreed upon definition of the word 'mind'. With all the studies in psychology and other disciplines, the word 'mind' has not yet been defined. And that is where the philosophical systems of India differ. We begin with the definition of the mind. I have spoken of this self as a force; the mind also is a particular type of force-field. It may be a weak force-field or a strong force-field. It may be a scattered one or it may be a concentrated one. And this is a force-field, which is centred and not spread out. When the entire mind is concentrated into a single point and that mind becomes a point, like the first brilliant point of light from which the whole universe emanates, when your entire mind force becomes in itself a point, then it is called a 'one-pointed mind'.

I have been working on the preparations, but being a man of very high ambitions, one day I hope to have a one-pointed mind, that is, when my entire force-field called the mind will be concentrated at a single point — a point that has no magnitude, and by not having magnitude, it becomes the gateway to burst into the realm of infinity. And that in the *tantric* tradition is called *bindu-bhedan*, bursting through the point.

The history of the universe is the history of the mind; the creation of the universe is the creation of the mind. In the traditions of India, when we speak of creation, we first speak of the creation of mind. So the mind is not something that is produced from the combination of biochemical forces. God first created the mind, and that is the universal mind, just as in our individual personality, we have our force-field called the mind and the body is governed by it. In the universe, firstly there is the mind and the visible tangible universe is its body, with all its different limbs. The mind that is first created is an enlightened mind. It is not a mind that has yet identified itself with the tangible, physical forms of matter. There is something I am leaving out here about the definition of mind, which I will clarify later. I do not want to make it too complicated right now. When we speak of the enlightened mind, the most common word for it is the word *guru* — the first universal mind that is the enlightened mind, otherwise known as *hiranya garbha* or the golden womb. That is the first *guru*, who is not a being or form; it is the universal mind, the enlightened mind of the universe.

How many buckets of water can you take out of the ocean? In how many mirrors can you catch the reflection of the sun? Into how many lakes can the reflection of the full moon fall at night? Accordingly this one single universal mind diversifies itself. The first process of diversification that occurs is the birth of the original beings, the *rishis* or the founders of the science of yoga. The first founders of the meditative tradition are not human beings; they are the minds that have not yet been embodied. Thereafter, as the process of creation unfolds, they become embodied. Becoming embodied, they remain enlightened. As further diversification continues subsequently, all living beings arise. But deep within themselves they are linked to that original enlightened mind which we call the *guru* within.

Many people sit with closed eyes and try to address the *guru* within, but what they actually connect with are the accumulations of their subconscious minds. The *guru* within is beyond the mind, beyond all mental processes. Normally, when people discuss meditation, they talk about the preparatory systems. These preparatory systems have developed over a period of time — not developed but unfolded — not unfolded but diversified from one single path of awareness.

In this personality, we have several gateways and layers of the path to that ultimate, or even the path to our own individual force-field called the mind. It is not a single path. We may go through any of the gateways. If we choose to go through the gateway of the eye, we learn to meditate on light. If we choose to go through the gateway of the ear, we learn to meditate on sound. How do we go through the gateway of the eye? Someone will give us a candle and ask us to do *trataka* or concentrate on that. Someone else will say you have seen a flame, you know what it looks like, so just think of that flame; let it be a mental flame. Depending on our grade, some people have to sit there and look at the flame for half an hour before they can remember what a flame looks like. Others can just close their eyes, and as they have seen the flame many times, they can just concentrate on this. Well, there are two eyes and with which one of the two eyes should I visualise the flame? No, no, not there; there is another place, so we name it the third eye. And then in that meditation, there are many different layers and levels. Or we can choose to go by the nostrils, using the way of the breath, and so on. Certain pathways are easier for a large number of people to enter through. The Himalayan tradition finds that the easiest way is through the awareness of the breath, but we will come to the reason for that later. Therefore, we seldom begin in our tradition with the meditation on light or concentration on sound or any other sense — experiences, memories, thoughts, or visualisations.

Speaking of masters, to be a master, one has to be a master of all the systems. Because to him, it is not many systems; it is just one system, just as having the eyes, skin, ears do not make us into three people. We are a composite being and these are our faculties. So a master has the fullest awareness of the forces active in all these pathways. A master knows where one system connects with another. The second thing about a master is that he may teach by uttering words from the mouth, but that is not the primary teaching. He may write down a technique; again that is not the primary technique. Due to the fact that he is linked to that primal mind I was speaking of earlier, through that mind, he connects directly with you. And through his presence, he brings your mind to a level of experience and then names it. In fact, when we train meditation teachers, we try to see whether a person through his presence can induce a state of meditation.

There are many different paths of meditation. Some say the *mantra* alone is enough and that is the way of groups, like trascendental meditation. Some say the breath alone is enough and that is the way of the Theravada Buddhists, including some schools of Vipassana and the Burma, Thailand, Cambodia, Laos systems. Their most popular schools emphasise on the breath alone, but there are those who maintain connection to the larger picture by combining the *mantra* and breath. The breath, the *mantra*, the light, the sound — each one has its specific place.

HISTORY OF MEDITATIVE TRADITIONS

While dwelling on the history of yoga and meditation, one can reflect on how long the practice of meditation has been cultivated and developed in the Himalayan mountains. The scale of the Himalayas spans the border of Burma to the border of Afghanistan; and from here to Kazakhstan, about 1,500 miles approximately east-west, and 500-800 miles in depth. Some of its highest mountain peaks have not been explored yet.

In these mountains, in these cave monasteries, *yogis* have sat for thousands of years. In the *Brihad Aranyaka Upanishad* or the *Upanishad* of the great forest dated 14th century BC, there is a list of sixty-nine generations of teachers as well as lists of who taught whom. Since then, the period of Gautam Buddha is another 800 years, and then Buddha to Jesus is another 600 years, and Jesus to Shankaracharya is another 800 years, and from then to now is another 1,200 years. Forgetting about these 1,972,000 years in terms of modern historians, we are talking about 5,000 to 6,000 years of the recorded line of teachers.

So, in these 5,000 to 6,000 years, what has been taught by these great ones, who did nothing but explore the self and consciousness, without any exterior props? One of the major ideas behind the entire practice of meditation is for the human being to discover what he is; not what he can do to the universe, or what he can do to change and destroy the forests or not even whether he can send man to the moon or to Mars. It's great that space explorations have made much progress through the touch of a human being, but what progress has the human being made? Can you change your breath from the right nostril to the left without any external aid? Can you calm your anger without the help of a psychologist? Can you lower your blood pressure without using any medicine? So, for the human consciousness to know itself, to be independent of matter, to be independent of physical props is one of the achievements of a meditator.

What can you do by yourself, within yourself? If there were no wheels on Earth and if human beings were to forget the art of weaving and wear no clothes, does it mean that among these human beings, no philosopher can arise? Why is it a precondition of a philosopher arising that man should have a can-opener rather than smashing a coconut on a stone? So one thing that I would like to see happen is to think of technology as a tool, and know that it is not a tool for human consciousness. They are not tools of human progress. The progress of a human being is within; what we do within ourself, without caring whether we walk around wrapped in a blanket or in polar fleece. So many great scholars pass by on this street looking like nothing. Hence, freedom from our conditioning, our dependence on the environment, is essential.

Now I am going to get a bit critical. "I can't meditate because there are too many people in the group." Wherever we are seated, no one else has sat there. In that space, no one else sits. Our continuity of time is very personal to us as no one else shares it. His or her continuity of time is his or her own. Whatever I have learned in my life meditatively, especially since I met my master twenty-seven years ago, half of that *sadhana* has been done sitting in American airports. Otherwise I have no time. So when driving from your home to the airport, how many breaths did you take? From my meditation centre in Minneapolis to the airport, it is thirty-four breaths, and that is how I have done my *sadhana*, sitting in the car on the way to the airports. Because 'will I catch the plane' or 'will I not catch the plane' — that anxiety has no bearing on whether or not I will catch the plane. So if it will not make any difference, why waste energy on something so non-productive? That is where the test of our meditation comes.

I promised to divulge the history of meditative traditions and the different paths of yoga. We will see how much we can cover in such a short book; the main thing is to get a sense of the philosophy as applicable to ourselves. While reading all the scriptures, I have found clues pertaining to the spread of the meditative tradition in all civilisations. Since mystics have a different language and they couch their words in such a way that only another mystic can understand what is being said, no one else can. It is a sort of cryptic language. "Jesus appeared to his disciples and he breathed into them." Unless a master has stood in front of you and breathed into you, you would not know what it means.

There are three pre-requisites before we are given the vows of *sanyasa*: to be above the desire for generation, to be above the desire for wealth, and to be above the desire for reputation, fame, and recognition. A true *yogi* does not seek fame and recognition; he makes himself available, makes himself known, but does not seek fame and recognition as that is not his benchmark of success. Thus wherever the *yogis* have gone, they have gone as chameleons. Here, I wear the robes of a traditional *swami*, whereas in the USA, I travel with my tie. Nobody would know. When I go to Buddhist countries, they think I am a Buddhist monk, and when I was in my whites before taking my vows of renunciation or sometimes held retreats in Catholic centres and so on, I was greeted with, "Come in Father, yes Father, no Father." Appearing as chameleons, the *yogis* have experienced all kinds of cultures, and since outward appearances are immaterial to them, they just merge in and come to the essentials. Whatever they find the most positive, they pick on that and work on that. It's a conspiracy.

What does the word 'conspiracy' mean? 'Con' means together and 'spirit' means 'to breathe'. The word must have arisen upon seeing a group of people sitting together in a catacomb or somewhere, when they were breathing together. Everyone gets afraid and paranoid seeing such a group and the conclaves of breathing together thus became known as a 'conspiracy'. We are all co-conspirators. The tradition travelled from there. The teachings of the *Upanishads* spread. There are records by Greek travellers from around the 1st century AD., when the teachers went out from here to China. I read somewhere that when Bodhidharma went to China, people were not ready to listen to him; so he sat facing a wall with a begging bowl at his side for eight or twelve years until he sensed that people were ready to listen to him. Later the Chinese teachers taught in Korea, followed by the Chinese and Korean teachers teaching in Japan. The *Yoga-sutra's* word for meditation is *dhyana*. The language spoken by Buddha is a vulgate form of Sanskrit, and is known as the Pali language — in that the word for meditation is *jnana*. Chinese is a monosyllabic language and the Chinese pronounce the word Ch'an; the Chinese teachers taught in Korea and pronounced it San; the Korean teachers taught it in Japan and they called it Zen. Now, people come to us and ask, "What is the difference between Zen meditation and your meditation?" It is like asking our great grandfather, what is the difference between us and our great grandchild? It is an ongoing tradition; this is one direction how the meditation system spread.

There was another group of teachers who crossed over to Central Asia and taught around the Caspian. They crossed into the Mongolian and Gobi Desert and went all the way into Siberia. The word Siberia is derived from the Sanskrit word *shivira*, which means a camp because everybody there camped, and they not only absorbed the meditative traditions, but also the traditions

of Ayurveda. I know someone, for example, who has retranslated
the ancient Ayurveda texts from Mongolian back into Sanskrit,
but which have been lost in India. And some of those traditions
are still continuing and being taught in the Buriyat Republic of
Russia, on Lake Baikal, earning it the title of the holy lake.

Traditions between the Greeks and the *yogis* also existed in
history. One of my favourite passages is from the Latin poet,
Ovid's, titled *Metamorphosis*. *Metamorphosis* is in fifteen cantos.
He writes of changes in human beings, like the story of Narcissus,
and how he turned into a flower at the riverbank. But in the last
chapter, the last canto of Ovid, the title of that chapter in Latin
is 'Nux', which means the 'walnut' because like the nut, the
human personality too contains so many segments. He speaks of
the quotes by Pythagoras and moving verses on reincarnation.
Nowadays in the West, when you think of reincarnation, you
think of human-to-human reincarnation. But one thing that both
Indians and the Greeks had in common was that there was no
differentiation between human and non-human life. The soul
was a soul and it could migrate from one form to another. That
still remains the belief here in India. Pythagoras so movingly
writes, "This animal whose throat you are slitting may have been
your grandmother in a previous life. Oh, you cruel human beings,
who have given up the ways of gods, have you got nothing else
left to eat but blood and gore?" But Pythagoras draws upon an
earlier tradition to which he refers — the tradition of Orpheus,
in which the view of the great Indian *yogi* Aurobindo is the same
as the Vedic *ribu*, and so you have many different historical and
geographical connections in the spread of the tradition of
meditation.

In European history, during the period from Constantine's

conversion to Christianity, all the way up to the 13th century, when the village of Albigens in south of France was obliterated, mention is made of the Christian church called the Manichean heresy. Mani was a prophet in the 3rd century AD, who was born in Iran, which was at that time a Zoroastrian country. He studied and practiced in India, went back and declared that he was the joint incarnation of Buddha, Zarathushtra and Jesus. One day, I was talking about this to one of my disciples in Canada, and she asked me, "Is it possible?" I said, "What is possible?" And she said, "To be the joint reincarnation of three?" And I said, "Three; what three?"

Continuing Mani's tale, the rest of the people who did believe in numerals didn't like it. "Declare yourself whether you are a Christian, a Buddhist, or a Zoroastrian," and they persecuted him. He suffered the fate of the prophet. Finally, the Zoroastrian priest was killed. But his religion had already spread very far. The remains of his teachings are found all the way from China through Central Asia, through Europe and right through Egypt. From 3rd century AD to the 13th century, it was one of the major religions in the world, with millions of followers. They were believers of reincarnation and were vegetarian. So this fad about how everybody in the USA is turning vegetarian is nothing new. It has all been done before. It is a revival of old Western traditions, the vegetarianism of Pythagoras, and the vegetarianism of the Manicheans. And finally when these Manicheans were so hunted and persecuted, one small pocket remained in the south of France in the village of Albigens, to be destroyed around the 13th century. But the people from there scattered and carried on their activities underground. Three to four centuries later there suddenly emerged the movement of the Friends, the Quakers.

There is a slender thread separating the two and that thread never breaks. Quietly it comes up somewhere. The energy goes on; it flows on. It may cease to be collective, the communities may break up, the religions may be demolished, the churches may cease to be, the names may change, the garb that the priests wear may alter, and completely new languages may become dominant. Last century, French was the lingua franca of the Western world; today it is English. In future, people might look upon English as this ancient language. Somebody will stumble upon some manuscript somewhere after many wars that have devastated so many libraries and will try to find the key. They may find the word meditation and think, 'Oh, people meditated even 5,000 years ago.' It will be a wonderful discovery, a great discovery. If you are there, you will be able to share the excitement of the archaeologists and epigraphy experts.

Thus, the external forms keep changing. The Manichean meditation was mainly based on light. The text of the Manichean tradition has recently been unearthed and published as a German translation. In Buddhist meditation, there exist several branches, such as the Tibetan branch which is a merger of the *tantra* that reached there from here along the mountain ranges. When the Dalai Lama speaks, he speaks of this land as the *guru* and Tibet as the disciple. He has said this many times. As many as eighty-four *siddhas*, that the Tibetan and Indian *yogic* traditions hold in common, had spread the teachings there. They encountered the existing Bunpo religion, which was the indigenous Tibetan religion. In short, the Tibetan meditative tradition was formed by a merger of the Bunpo religion, the *tantra* and the Buddhist tradition. One of the features of Tibetan meditation is that it is very heavy on complex visualisations. They are not the kind of visualisations of free associations that psychologists associate with meditation in the West. The problem nowadays with meditation in the West is that when they undertake visualisations, people use their imagination. The problem with this imagination is that we tend to introduce our own mental association (I am using the term 'association' as per the psychological norms). And there can be psychological dangers in that because we are not a perfectly enlightened being. Our association with a word or image is not free of a load; it is not free of our own personal unconscious connections, so it has nothing to do with our intuition.

Intuition is something completely free of psychological associations. Intuition, in order to be pure intuition, should not arise out of our personal psychology. And no one is equipped to detect the difference between what is arising from our own psychological association and what is arising from spiritual intuition, from the *atman*, the self. So, I do not teach the free association kind of visualisations. But the Tibetan visualisations are very systematic, very methodical, as they do not refer to psychological associations. They refer to the archetypes; not the limitations imposed on the archetypes by the individual consciousness. Note the difference between the two. Going down south, there is the Thai, the Theravada Buddhist meditation, with its own emphasis, but people think that in the Theraveda, there are no visualisations. But that is not true. For example, if we read *Visuddhi Maga*, the main text in Theravada Buddhism, the path of purification, which gives the systematic meditation in Theravada, of the southern branch of Buddhism that is followed in Burma and Thailand, the same text has a different version in Sri Lanka and is known as *Vimuthi Maga*. There are several different schools of the southern branch of Buddhism. China has two different systems, one direct from India and one from Tibet. And again there are three or four systems that merge in China — the Tao merges with Buddhist meditation — that is one system in which the Chinese gods, the Jade Emperor and so on, get identified with some of the Buddhist deities, and a superimposition occurs. Then there exists one branch of Ch'an meditation which is more akin to the Vedanta meditation. People have heard of yoga meditation, but most have not heard of Vedanta meditation. Let me explain the difference: when we speak of yoga meditation, the meditative path in Tibetan Buddhism means preparation of the body; also in Tao, which is very similar to *tantra*. We cannot differentiate in China how much is Tao and how much is *tantra*, and how much is the Indian *tantra*, and how much is the Tibetan *tantra*, as it is all a complete merger. There exists a system of preparing the body, concentrating on the breath, using a *mantra* and so on. It entails purely the use of intellect to make a breakthrough. That is the path of *jnana yoga*. The path of *kriya yoga* is derived from the Patanjali and *tantra* systems. The path of *bhakti yoga*, the path of devotion, again originally derived from Patanjali's *Ishwara Pranitana*, emphasises on the presence of God. The path of *karma yoga* or yoga of action, taught in the *Bhagavad Gita*, and in the book of Tao, *Tao Te Ching*, or in such practices in diverse traditions, such as in Zen, involves meditating while using the body. Meditation in gardening, in creating a rock garden, all of that comes under *karma yoga*, i.e. meditating while performing actions. It is not just performing actions. Meditating while waiting for a bus is *karma yoga*, and so it is meditating while answering the phone. My *ashram* staff laughs as they hear this every day and they are tired of it. That is *karma yoga*. And *jnana yoga* is not reading books. *Jnana yoga* is using purely the intellect to make a breakthrough to go beyond intellect.

THE TAO PATH

Tao exists in two forms: the mythological form of Tao that you see in the Taoist temple, with all the deities and sages of the Tao tradition, and the pure Tao of practices, that are absolutely the same as the *tantra* tradition of bringing concentration on the breath, mastery of the sex urge and the practice of celibacy. It was an independent development in China. In fact, we have *tantras* that say that this particular *tantra* is derived from the Chinese tradition. I have in my library Sanskrit texts that are titled *Tantra* as taught in Greater China. Sage Vashishta brought the Chinese tradition to India, indicating that there has been a continuous exchange. There was greater communication in those days than there is now. In Vedanta, *jnana yoga* is concentration on and analysis of the four *mahavakyas*. The major ones are four, but there are ones that are lesser known. I know up to thirty-two, but there may be more. *Mahavakya*, which means the 'great sentence', are short, selected passages from the *Upanishadic* texts. For example, when we take our vows of renunciation, depending on our order, for each of the orders a specific *mahavakya* is given. Just as we give *mantras* secretly in initiation, the initiator in the Vedanta tradition which we represent because of our descent from the Shankaracharya lineage, a secret *mahavakya* is also shared. Whereas *mantra* is for meditation, *mahavakya* is used for contemplation. How do we use that for analysis? Take the *mahavakya*, 'Tat tvam asi' (I am that). Analyse that sentence and you analyse it in a personal context, eliminating the lesser and lesser, the lower and lower findings, to go on to the higher and higher findings until that becomes the experience. That is a methodical way of doing it and even in the Vedantic monasteries, just as in the Christian monasteries, there are many great scholars who teach the *Upanishads*; there are very few who know the actual way of contemplation. Here it may be noted that the same meditation is not given to everybody or the same path is shown to everybody. Now, the first question in Vedanta is, 'Who am I?' The picture we see of ourself today, is ours. If we see a picture of ours when we were born, that is also ours. But actually which one of the two is us? That's a simple example. So whatever we identify with is not us. The path of Ramana Mahrashi was based on the question, 'Who am I?' Not surprisingly, out of the 1,700 paradoxical sentences which are given in the Ch'an tradition to contemplate, the first one is; 'Who am I?' The Chinese term *kungan*, the source of the Japanese word *koan* is a way of enquiring 'Who am I?' The same is in Vedanta, and it goes on progressively. We may have read some of the *koans*, of the Japanese Zen tradition, and some of them are the same as the ones in the Chinese Ch'an system, but some are different. So we have this set of paradoxical statements, in which we have to resolve the paradox. And the same path of *jnana yoga* goes on in the path of *koan*. In Zen, we find the combination of breath practice on one side and the practice of *koan* at the same time, and there are certain paths in Zen which also give *mantras*. They are not well known but they are there. *Namo* is actually the Japanese corruption of the Sanskrit — *Namo amitbahasya*.

The Sanskrit language, which was the classical language of India, and up to the 19th century it was thought to be the mother of all the Indo-European languages, is now considered a senior sister of ancient Greek and Latin. By the historical dating system of modern scholars, the earliest Sanskrit texts are 4,000-years old. Nearly seventy per cent of Sanskrit literature is not yet published; it is in the form of manuscripts in India. What exists in Thailand,

Cambodia and Japan and in other countries is a whole different dimension. The original Sanskrit script known as *Brahmi* has given rise to three different script traditions in Asia: the Sanskrit tradition, the Chinese tradition, and the Hebraic tradition, which include the Arabic and Ethiopian scripts that are written from right to left. There are about twenty different scripts used in India, even now in modern times. The script of Tibet, Burma, Laos, Cambodia, old Vietnam and all the old different scripts of the Kavi language in Indonesia and the pre-Spanish invasion scripts used in the Phillippines are derived from the same Sanskrit script. Even on the main gate of the Great Wall of China, where it opens to Mongolia, there are inscriptions in Sanskrit. The problem was that *mantras* could not be written in Chinese. Wherever you find these scripts derived from the Brahmi script, there is a meditative tradition. The Christian meditation has one thing in common with the Tibetan meditation — it has the visualisations of a deity, as Jesus on the cross. It is in a simplified form, but if the same method is taught properly, and the other has lot in common with *jnana yoga*, that is if we take a passage from the scriptures, we shall say that now we will meditate on this passage. This is a very commonly known system even now. *Jnana yoga* is found in all the different paths. Only the historical and geographical picture is given here but the interior geography has a whole map of human consciousness, and in that map of human consciousness, as in the *tantra* system, we have the three *nadis* — *ida, pingala, sushumna*, the breath, and so on. The one main *nadi*, the *sushumna*, the three main *nadis* — the *ida, pingala, sushumna*, the ten main *nadis*, next step, fourteen *nadis*, next step, 72,000 energy currents, next step, 325,000 *nadis*, next step, and 350 million *nadis*. Each of these have been explored by the masters.

CHAPTER 2

BEGINNING MEDITATION

Common to the practices of many schools, the first step to meditation is essentially awareness of breathing.

In this section, I would like to offer the first-level instruction in the method of meditation that anyone can start and practice at any time anywhere. It is seldom to be found in books and even when suggested in books, it is seldom properly understood. Yet it is so simple that I have found even a three-year-old child can take to it.

STEPS IN THE METHOD

I give here a systematic point-to-point method of starting the practice. Anyone at any age can begin: the younger the better. On the other hand, it is never too late in life. Starting even during a terminal illness would be helpful and may prolong life; at least it will impart peace. The practice should be done at least once a day, for whatever length of time is available.

It is not in the length of the period of meditation that success lies, but in intensifying the awareness, which comes gradually. One may also practice it at other times of the day, when one is tired and needs a quick recovery of energy; when one gets angry or frustrated and wants to be gentler; when one is busy and consequently tense and needs to relax so one can be more effective. One may do it while waiting at the airport, a railway station, or in a car when someone else is driving. There is no restriction and no limit. No harm can ever come from this practice.

In the *Raja Yoga* meditation system, as taught by the Himalayan *yogis*, the various steps of meditation constitute the foundation. The reader's ego may want to say: 'I have been practicing meditation for a decade or two. I want something more advanced. I do not need elementary lessons.' This attitude is incorrect.

Many aspirants practice while blanking out the mind, or holding the breath like an athlete, but they have not learnt the correct method of breathing. In our system, we check everyone on the following points, and only when these foundations have been properly laid do we proceed any further.

The steps in the method are:

- Diaphragmatic and uniform breathing
- Correct posture, with a straight spine, and no feeling of discomfort in the legs, back or the neck. One should be able to maintain such a correct and straight position of the spine without encountering discomfort
- *Shithili-karana* or systematic relaxation is essential. One should maintain total relaxation of the neuro-muscular system throughout the meditation session
- Awareness of breathing has some subtler modes that one learns gradually
- Using a *mantra* or a sacred word from whichever spiritual tradition: (a) initially a sound that flows easily with the

breath, such as the word *so-ham*; (b) after such a step has been mastered, a *mantra-diksha* (initiation into *mantra*) is given and more advanced methods of refined *japa* (mental remembrance of the *mantra*) are gradually introduced

Let us go into the details of these steps.

DIAPHRAGMATIC BREATHING

The chief organ controlling the breathing process in our body is the diaphragm, which is a muscle just underneath the ribs, separating the chest cavity from the abdomen. Ideally, the diaphragm contracts so that we may inhale fully even into the lower lungs. The diaphragm relaxes to push against the lower lungs so that exhalation from this part of the lungs may be completed. A child at birth breathes diaphragmatically but later forgets this natural process. One has to re-train oneself to breathe correctly.

In deep and correct breathing, no pressure should be felt in the lungs and no tension should develop. Breathing should be relaxed so that a feeling of rejuvenation is experienced.

Diaphragmatic breathing is taught in (a) *makarasana*, the crocodile position or lying on one's stomach, and is practiced further in (b) *shavasana*, the corpse position, as well as in sitting and standing positions.

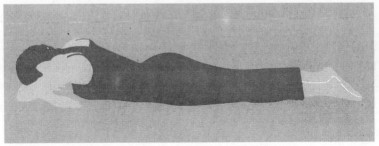

(a) *makarasana*

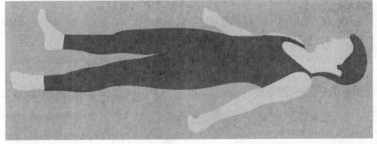

(b) *shavasana*

To learn the practice, lie on the stomach with the heels touching and toes apart, or in whatever way the legs feel relaxed. Bend the elbows, place the right palm down over the back of the left hand, and rest the forehead on the hands. The neck is not to be bent sideways. Let the shoulders relax.

Bring your awareness to the breathing process. In this position, it is not possible to do chest breathing. Observe the flow of the breath. Observe the gentle rise and fall of the stomach and the navel area with the smooth flow of the breath.

Let there be no jerks, no breaks, in your breathing. Let it flow like a smooth stream. Let it slow down. Observe the gentle flow, along with the rise and fall of the stomach and the navel area. Take note of the breathing process. Resolve to breathe in this way at all times.

After doing this practice for five to fifteen minutes, turn over on your back in the *shavasana* position. Continue to breathe and observe the process of the diaphragm relaxing and contracting (the rise and fall of the stomach and the navel area).

Place your left palm on the chest, right palm on the stomach. No movement should be felt under the left palm; the right palm should feel the rise and fall smoothly, without a jerk, without a break.

Let uniform breathing develop, the length of the inhalation and the exhalation being equal. When this practice has been mastered, one graduates to 2:1 breathing (where exhalation is twice as long as inhalation), but not right now.

When one breathes only diaphragmatically at all times, it is considered that the practice has been mastered.

CORRECT POSTURE

It is most important that your spine should be kept straight when sitting in meditation and ideally at all other times.

Unfortunately, all chairs, sofas, modern beds, car seats and airplanes are designed to force people to breathe incorrectly by making them sit with convoluted spines.

One often sees people sitting in prayer, in *kathas*, and in *satsangs*, with their spines looking sadly like a bent bow. This firstly prevents correct and full breathing, causing short breaths and reducing the life span and secondly, it generates or worsens many diseases such as those of the spine.

A straight spine is not a straight line. It is a slightly S-shaped curve, convex at the lower-third part (lumbar vertebrae, one to five), concave at the middle-third part (thoracic vertebrae two to twelve); convex at the upper part of the back (cervical vertebrae five to thoracic vertebrae one); and straight at the neck (cervical vertebrae one to four).

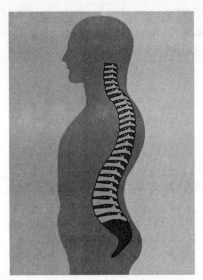

It should be learnt under expert guidance. But a few hints here will be helpful. One need not try to sit in the advanced postures like *siddhasana* and *padmasana*, especially if age, physical problems, or lack of habit prevents one from doing so. Sitting in a chair or sitting in a comfortable cross-legged position will do quite nicely.

Unfortunately, when people sit in the cross-legged position, the centre of gravity makes them bend their backs. The answer to that is a simple one.

Fold a blanket and make it into a neat and firm cushion. It is not to serve as your seat, not like a rug to sit on. Place it only under the hip bones, with legs or knees on the floor. This will uplift the hips from the ground. Straighten yourself. If there is discomfort anywhere in the back or the neck, you need to experiment with the height of the cushion under the hips by reducing or increasing the number of folds in the blanket. Experiment for a few days till you obtain optimum comfort. Resolve always to sit in this position.

If sitting on the floor is very difficult, you may sit in *mitrasana* — on the edge of a hard chair, with the feet on the ground. But do sit with the spine straight. Form this habit. Let it become your natural position at all times. You will notice psychological changes in yourself, such as heightened awareness, intentness, self-confidence without unnecessary pride and effectiveness in life.

Having sat in the correct posture, continue breathing diaphragmatically with mental observation of the flow, and of the gentle rise and fall of the stomach and the navel area, without any pressure in the chest. If there is tension, the form of breathing is incorrect.

SYSTEMATIC RELAXATION

Shithilikarana, after diaphragmatic breathing, is the second step practiced in *shavasana.* There are numerous progressively complex mental exercises done in *shavasana,* which finally lead to *yoga-nidra,* and to entry into the subtle body.

Let us learn here how to practice the basic relaxation method. Lie in *shavasana,* with feet apart, arms separate from the body, alongside the body, palms up. Continue breathing diaphragmatically. Now, take a mental inventory of your body in the following sequence, asking each part of the body to relax as it is brought to the mind.

Forehead, eyebrow, eyes, nostrils, cheeks, jaw and the corners of your mouth, chin, neck, neck joint, shoulders, shoulder joints, upper arms; elbows, lower arms, wrists, hands, fingers, fingertips; fingertips, hands, wrists, lower arms, elbows, upper arms, shoulder joints, shoulders, chest, heart area, stomach, navel, abdomen, pelvis, thigh joints, thighs, knees, calf muscles, ankles, feet and toes.

Now in the reverse order go up the body as follows:

Toes, feet, ankles, calves, knees, thighs, thigh joints, pelvis, abdomen, navel, stomach, heart area, chest, shoulders, shoulder joints, upper arms, elbows, lower arms, wrists, hands, fingers, fingertips; fingertips, fingers, hands, wrists, lower arms, elbows, upper arms, shoulder joints, shoulders, neck joint, neck, chin, jaw, corners of your mouth, cheeks, nostrils, eyes, eyebrows, forehead.

Remember this sequence. Go over the body in this order, relaxing each of these parts in this sequence. Let them go limp. For example, the hands should become like the hands of a baby. If you do not succeed in relaxing them at first, or you are so tense that you forget what it is like for a muscle to be relaxed, you may use a different method of relaxation called tension relaxation, which is also done in *shavasana*.

The exact sequence for practicing this relaxation exercise is as follows. When tensing the muscles, be tense by beginning from the fingers or toes upward. Try to avoid sympathetically tensing of muscles other than the ones you are working with. Between segments, pause and relax for two breaths. After completing the entire sequence, rest for ten relaxed breaths.

- Tense and relax the right leg — left leg — right leg — left leg

- Tense and relax both the legs simultaneously. Repeat
- Tense and relax the right leg and arm — left leg and arm — right leg and arm — left leg and arm
- Tense and relax the right arm — left arm — right arm — left arm; then both arms simultaneously. Repeat
- Tense and relax all the limbs simultaneously. Repeat

After completing either the body sequence relaxation or the tension relaxation, continue breathing diaphragmatically, with observation as described earlier. Lie in this position for a few minutes, then sit up for meditation. Do remember to sit with the seat bones resting on a folded blanket, and with the spine straight.

Again, quickly scan the body for any sign of tension that might have developed in the process of changing the position. Relax. Re-establish diaphragmatic breathing.

BREATH AWARENESS

Let your breath flow, smoothly and evenly, with no jerks, no break in the middle of the breath, no break between the breaths, no sound, no gasping. It should be like *tailadharavat*, like a smooth stream of oil being poured. Become aware of the flow with no break in the awareness.

Feel the flow and touch of the breath in the nostrils. Continue to do so, without jerk, without interruption. The awareness of inhalation should immediately merge into the awareness of exhalation and vice versa. The awareness of exhalation is especially important.

If the mind wanders off, because of its usual habit that has been given to it over many lifetimes, straighten your spine again. Relax quickly again and re-establish diaphragmatic breathing while continuing with the awareness of the flow and touch of the breath in the nostrils.

MANTRA OR SACRED WORD

To begin with, use *so-ham*, while some prefer to say *hamso* and call it the *hamsa-mantra*. Exhaling, mentally remember the word *ham*. Inhaling mentally, remember the word *so*. It means, 'I am that'. Those in a different religious tradition may use the word prescribed by their tradition, but it should be properly learnt from someone who knows meditation according to *that* tradition. Those in the Himalayan tradition are trained to teach according to each person's religious (or atheist) background.

Let there be no interruptions in breath awareness, or in the awareness of the flow of the word as thought. Observe how the breath, the word and the mind flow together as a single stream.

Slowly, lengthen the time — not how long you sit — but how many seconds you manage to maintain awareness of the flow of that stream without interruption. Too much effort is self-defeating. One cannot fall asleep by making a determined effort, nor can one enter a meditative state by fighting oneself. Let it flow; let it happen. Don't *do* meditation. Observe and experience.

MANTRA-DIKSHA

The next step is to seek out someone to give you the first initiation, or *mantra-diksha*, which is often referred to as a personal *mantra*. After the *mantra* initiation, one may be led to methods of meditation individually appropriate for the aspirant. Both a *mantra* and a meditation mode are assigned according to the individual's *samskaras*, imprints in the unconscious gathered over many lifetimes, spiritual needs, and his *adhikara* or level of qualification. There are many different ways of refining the *mantra* experience through various *koshas*, sheaths, within the personality, all the way to final silence. The *ajapa* state also occurs through the *guru's* grace in which the mental remembrance of listening to the *mantra* ceases to be an act and becomes an experience occurring naturally, of its own accord.

One may be taught to proceed on the path of *nada* (internal sound) or *jyoti* (light) and to go on the path of the *kundalini* (a yoga of channelling energies). One may be assigned a particular *chakra*, centre of consciousness, to meditate on from time to time, but the entry into such meditation occurs only when the initiator mentally touches the disciple's particular *chakra*.

In the *chakra*, one may be assigned a visualisation on a certain diagram or object, or the presence of an *ishta devata*, one's favourite or chosen form of the deity, for example, Jesus or Mary for Christians, Buddha for the Buddhists, and so on. At this time, the aspirant will also be taught how to merge his *mantra* with the energy of the given *chakra* and how to penetrate through its *bindu-bhedan* (central point). The secrets of these practices are taught in specific *tantras* but understood only in the live *guru*-disciple relationship. The Himalayan tradition means transmission of consciousness in a direct preceptor-student mutual presence.

SEQUENTIAL STEPS IN LEARNING TO BREATHE DIAPHRAGMATICALLY

Diaphragmatic breathing in crocodile position

To learn to breathe correctly and to learn to relax by using the correct way of breathing, lie on your stomach, cross your arms, or put one hand on the other, and rest your forehead on the arms, or the hand without bending your neck.

- Keep your toes touching, your heels apart, and ankles practically flat on the ground; your shoulders flat; your armpits practically touching the ground

- Bring your attention away from all other places and be aware of only the place where you are lying down
- Be aware of only the space that your body occupies from head to toe
- Now become aware of the flow of your breath. Observe the flow of your breath, as though your breath is flowing through your whole body from top to toes and toes to top
- Breathe gently, slowly, smoothly with no jerk or break in your breathing. Exhale all your tension and stress, inhaling a feeling of fullness, relaxation, peace and purity
- Now bring your attention to the gentle rise and fall of your stomach and the navel area. Observe how that area gently lifts from the ground as you exhale and how it gently touches the ground as you inhale
- Observe that movement with the gentle rhythm of your breath. This is known as diaphragmatic breathing — no breaks, no jerks
- Continue to observe the rise and fall of the stomach and navel area, with the gentle rhythm of your breathing Observe which muscles move to constitute that movement and by observing that, learn to breathe correctly, so that you may always breathe in this manner

You may lie in this position as long as you normally wish. Continue to breathe this way, taking note of how the movement occurs along with your breathing.

In corpse position

Now, gently roll over and lie on your back with your feet apart, arms separate from the body, alongside the body and the back of the hand resting on the ground.

- Let your entire body relax and again continue to breathe as you were breathing in the crocodile position
- Observe the gentle rise and fall of the stomach and navel area
- Observe how that area gently relaxes and slightly inflates as you inhale and contracts as you exhale
- Place your left palm in the centre of your bosom. Place your right palm on your stomach between the sternum and the navel and continue to breathe as before
- Observe that there is no movement under the left palm on the chest. The movement should be felt only under the right palm
- As you exhale and inhale, gently observe the flow of your breath — no jerks in your breathing; no breaks
- You may lie in this position, observing the flow of your breath for ten to twenty minutes and two or three times a day for complete relaxation
- One way to quickly relax your body and mind is in this way
- Do this practice for five minutes, or even less or more as convenient at any time — wherever you are, sitting on a sofa, on an office chair, in a bus, in a car, in a meeting, or alone

Either of the two exercises, or both in sequence, for ten to twenty minutes two or three times a day, will change the texture and tone of your life in many ways.

Three-minute relaxation for the very busy

- Bring your attention only to the place where you are seated
- Be aware of only the space that your body is occupying from head to toe

- Be aware of only this moment in time
- Very quickly, relax your forehead
- Relax the eyebrows and eyes
- Relax your nostrils
- Relax your cheeks, jaw, and corners of your mouth
- Relax your chin, neck and shoulders
- Relax all the way down to the fingertips
- Relax from your fingertips to your shoulders
- Relax your chest, stomach, navel and abdomen
- Relax your thighs, calves, feet and toes
- Again relax all the organs from the toes upward and bring your awareness to your breathing
- Observe the gentle rise and fall of your stomach and navel area: how that area gently relaxes as you exhale, how it slightly expands as you inhale
- Observing this, feel the flow and touch of your breath in your nostrils

While exhaling, count in your mind o...n...e, inhaling t...w...o, exhaling t...h...r...e...e..., inhaling f...o...u...r, exhaling f...i...v...e, inhaling f...i...v...e, exhaling four, inhaling three, exhaling two, inhaling one; continue to count your breath from one through five and five through one. Feel the flow and the touch of your breath in your nostrils, breathing slowly, gently and smoothly.

- No break in your breathing; no break in your counting, one to five and five to one. Maintain the count
- Feel the flow and the touch of the breath in the nostrils, and continue the practice as long as you wish, and as frequently as you like
- Without breaking the count, gently open your eyes

One-minute meditation with *so-ham mantra*

- Simply be aware of yourself from head to toe
- Draw around yourself, as it were, three circles of light
- Resolve that the mind shall not cross these three circles, nor will any intruding thoughts and impressions enter from outside
- Remaining aware of yourself from head to toe, in just a few exhalations, relax all your limbs
- Your inhalation is for the purpose of exhalation, so inhale in order to exhale
- In each exhalation, progressively relax your entire body
- Now resolve that for the next one minute no other thought will arise except for awareness of the movement of your stomach and navel area, with the gentle rhythm of your breathing. Maintain that resolve for one minute
- Promise that for one minute there will be no other thought except the awareness of the path of your breath from the navel to the nostrils, nostrils to the navel. Only feel the breath flow on this path, maintaining the resolve
- Now feel the flow and the touch of your breath in your active nostril, but first resolve that for one minute there will be no intruding thought; only the feel of the flow of the breath in your active nostril
- Now resolve that for one minute there will be no intruding thought except the feel of the breath in your passive nostril
- Resolve that for one minute there will be no other thought except the feel of the breath in your two nostrils
- Now with your breath, exhale, thinking of the word *h...a...a..m...m* and inhaling the word, *soooo*

Resolve that for the next two minutes there will be no other thought except the feel of the breath in both the nostrils — inhaling with *soooo*, exhaling with *haaaammm*.

Maintain that resolve so that no break occurs between the exhalations and inhalations. Resolve for an additional two minutes that while feeling the breath and the word, you will observe how the mind and the word flow together as a single stream, the mind stream itself becoming the word and the breath and maintaining the resolve for two minutes. Now eliminate all dualities of the left and right; come to the *sushumna* breath. Mentally feel the spot where the nose bridge ends and the upper lip begins; also mentally feel the spot between the eyebrows.

- Inhale as though you were inhaling from the spot in front of the nose bridge a subtle energy flow to the spot between the eyebrows while exhaling the same way
- Maintain the same stream of the mind, word, and the energy flow
- This flow between the two spots is known as *sushumna* breath
- Resolve that for one minute there will be no other thought — only the feel of the flow of the stream in the *sushumna* channel
- Now using the centre between the eyebrows as the gateway, enter the chamber of your mind and resolve for a quarter minute or half a minute that there will be no exterior thought; only utter silence as though your mind becomes a lake of silence, absolutely still, without a ripple
- Resolve and maintain the enjoyment of such stillness and silence for a half a minute. Now from that lake of silence, come again through the gateway between the eyebrows

and resolve for one minute to be only in the *sushumna* breath

- Maintain the same stream, without the intrusion of any other thought

- Now continue in silence. Only a single ripple arises in the silent stillness of the lake of the mind, and that is the *so-ham mantra* in the breath

- Every two to three minutes or five minutes, renew the resolve to permit no other exterior thought

- If you have difficulty with that, you may practice the entire process that you have just gone through, in repeated segments and in the steps described. Sit as long as you wish

CHAPTER 3

KNOWING THE HIMALAYAN TRADITION

The Himalayan mountains have been the home of sages for millennia. These great sages lived and passed on the knowledge of *yogic* teachings to their disciples, who in turn became masters, passing on the teachings in an unbroken lineage since the Vedic period. Nealy 1,200 years ago, Shankaracharya organised his teachings into five centres of the Himalayan tradition. As one of those five, our tradition is the *Bharati* lineage. *Bha* means 'the light of knowledge', and *rati* means 'a lover who is absorbed in it'. Thus, *Bharati* indicates one, who as a lover of knowledge, becomes totally absorbed in its light. The methods and philosophies of the Himalayan tradition have withstood the test of time. Generation after generation has followed this path and a huge reserve of knowledge has been built.

The Himalayan tradition is not a tradition where a teacher proclaims himself a *guru* and the students are expected to believe whatever he says; rather, the teachings come from the tradition and the student can look to the tradition to support and make sense of what the teacher says. The initial purpose of the tradition is to awaken the divine flame within each human being and the goal is for each student to become a master of the tradition in coming to know his or her true self. It is the task of the teacher, through the grace of the *guru* to selflessly help his disciples on the path of highest enlightenment. Passing on of knowledge is done experientially through the transmission of a pulsation of energy.

The Himalayan tradition of yoga meditation combines the wisdom of Patanajali's *Yoga-sutras*, the philosophy and practices of the *tantra*, and the specific oral instructions and initiatory experiences, passed on by a long line of saints and yoga masters whose names may or may not be known. The tradition is not an intellectual combining of three unrelated elements, but a unified system in which all the parts are integrally linked.

The principal tenets and practices of all known systems of meditation are included in the Himalayan tradition and, for the most part, these systems have arisen out of it. For example, Vipassana emphasises breath awareness and transcendental meditation concentrates on the repetition of a *mantra*, whereas most *hatha* practitioners pay attention mainly to posture. The Himalayan meditator, however, learns to sit in the correct posture, relaxes fully, practices correct breathing, and then combines breath-awareness with the *mantra*.

When one reaches the end of the practices prescribed in any one of the Himalayan systems, continuity is to be found in the system as a whole. This statement may be explained this way: rare is a disciple who can master all the components of the Himalayan system, but he may master one or two aspects and be sent out to teach. He will draw students who are at the level of development where they can benefit from the system he has to offer. In this way, various schools of meditation have branched off from the central one. When students reach the ultimate end of the methods taught in any particular subsystem, their next step will be to follow the other aspects of the Himalayan system. This is termed as divergence and convergence of the meditational systems.

The chief components of the Himalayan system are purification of thoughts and emotions. To prevent internal disturbances from extraneous thoughts and sentiments arising during meditation, one needs to practice purification, such as:

- The five *yamas* — non-violence, truthfulness, non-stealing, abstinence from sensual indulgence, non-possessiveness, and the five *niyamas* (duties) — purity, contentment, practices that lead to perfection of body, mind and senses, study that leads to knowledge of the self and surrender to the Ultimate Reality
- The four *brahma-viharas* (right attitudes) — friendliness toward the happy, compassion for the unhappy, delight in the virtuous, and indifference towards the wicked
- The antidotes to *pratipaksha-bhavana* (disturbing thoughts) to *vi-tarkas* (ward off) the thoughts opposed to the *yamas, niyamas, and brahma-viharas* and so on. The practice of these leads to:
  - ethical behaviour
  - loosening of the bonds of *karma*
  - *chitta-pra-sadana,* clarity and purification of the mind, making the mind pleasant and clear
  - *sthiti-ni-bandhana,* firming up the physical, mental stability and steadiness in life and during meditation

It is not as simple as it appears. For example, the

preceptors of the Himalayan tradition state that they are able to sit in one posture for long hours because they are emotionally stable and undisturbed

* practise special *mantras* and *tantric* concentrations after having been initiated into states energising the *muladhara-chakra*. Just reading a scholarly commentary on the *Yoga-sutras* or *asanas* will not help the disciple to reach such a state; the entire integral system must be followed. For example, if one has mastered a meditation posture through *hatha* practices and can maintain that posture for some time, it will not prevent the practitioner from feeling a sensation of moving and swaying, etc. that many meditators suffer from

* the conquest of the *vikshepas* (the nine disturbances) in the path of concentration — sickness, mental laziness, doubt, lack of enthusiasm, sloth, craving for sensual pleasure, false perception, despair caused by failure to concentrate and unsteadiness in concentration and their accompaniments — grief, despondency, trembling of the body and irregular breathing. Without such a conquest one will remain bound to the first three states of the mind — *kshipta* (turbulent), *mudha* (stupefied), *vikshepas vi-kshipta* (distracted) and will not be able to move to the *bhumi* (next ground), *ekagra* (concentration) and *ni-ruddha* (totally controlled) in *samadhi*

For the conquest of these distractions, special methods are employed in the Himalayan oral tradition. For example, the involuntary physical movement or sensation of swaying even without a perceptible movement is overcome by

• purifying the emotions
• certain *mantras*

- meditating in the preceptor's presence which helps to steady the *sadhaka's* mind

Mindfulness: The practice of *smrty-upa-sthana* (Buddhist *sati-patthana*) takes many forms, the details of which are taught through personal instruction. For example, the Himalayan tradition teaches the method of *asanas* coupled with full awareness of the states of the body, breath and mind in a detailed methodology. In fact a major component in the practice of postures is self-awareness, deep self-observation, in all states of the body, breath and especially the mind.

Breath awareness: It starts as a part of mindfulness and becomes specialised as the very first step in the practice of meditation. Here, it is essential to learn diaphragmatic breathing that is slow, smooth, without jerks and without a break between the breaths. The living Himalayan tradition of meditation does not encourage practices like *kumbhaka*. It teaches the disciple to simply

- learn to breathe correctly in a manner conducive to meditation
- observe the breath flow which has many variations, (practicing for a long time without changing the technique)
- wait for *kevala-kumbhaka* to occur naturally when the mind, woven with the very subtle breath, comes to a standstill and thereby brings the breath to a suspended state

The practice of breath awareness branches off into many other modes of meditative experience, as given below:

Nadi-shodhana is purification of subtle energy channels. At least seven different forms of this category of *pranayama* that are performed include

- preparatory exercises such as seven different kinds of *bhastrikas* or bellows

- a number of variations to each of the seven channel-purifications may be practised

Pratyahara. It is the least understood of the *angas* (components) of yoga. If we understand the *sutra* correctly, it means:

- firstly calming the mind
- merging the senses into the calm/pacified/peaceful mind
- calming the sense faculties through certain breathing practices in which the awareness is centred on *pranamaya kosha*

Under a capable preceptor, one feels the movement of the *prana vayu* (subtle wind) moving from one point to another in the body in a systematic progression from point to point, until

- the physical body is forgotten
- the awareness of *pranamaya kosha* deepens
- the *prana* begins to merge into its source in the *manomaya kosha*, so that the mind is calmed and the senses are stilled. *Yoga-nidra* (not to be confused with simple *shavasana* practices that sometimes pass for *yoga-nidra*) is the next step, from which one may move towards the next step in *yoga-nidra* or towards deeper meditation, or practice both if one has the time for them

Kundalini breathing is the first step in the *tantric* path — the awareness of the energy flow in the spine, imagining and then feeling it, as though the breath is flowing through an imaginary hollow in the spine.

- Many uninitiated teachers nowadays try to teach *chakra* awakening without having first mastered the *sumeru pranayama*. Also, if one is not initiated by a master into this method, he cannot induce the experience of *sumeru* breathing

- If it is done without appropriate preparations, such as the correct way of maintaining the spine, it can lead to harm
- If it is done without using the appropriate *mantra* – not just any arbitrary *mantra* – one may not be able to channelise the energy, resulting in possible disturbances and diseases

Sa-garbha pranayama is commonly understood to mean the practice of *kumbhaka* with mental concentration on a *mantra*. The Himalayan system of *pranapana-smrti-upsthana* means the awareness of a *mantra* along with the awareness of the breath flow in all its various stages. Again, this is taught in an initiatory process. It also includes *japa*.

Japa: This is not simply a mechanical recitation of a *mantra* chosen at random. The science of *mantra* is based on an understanding of sound vibrations, which are primarily centred in the various points on the *kundalini* and cannot be grasped without initiation. The ultimate purpose of *japa* is to go into supreme silence. One first absorbs (the articulate level of speech) into *madhyama vaikhari* (the mental level). Then one silences even that and enters the realm of *pashyanti* (the vibration of revelation) such that one may become the channel for revelation. From there, one goes into the supreme absorption in the *para* (the transcendant) which is knowledge, as it exists in the divine principle. A preceptor trained in the Himalayan tradition leads into further refinements through nine major stages of *mantra* practice as taught in the *tantric* system.

Some of the variations of *japa* practice are as follows:

- Practising the *mantra* with awareness of the breath flow
- Practising the *mantra* while performing daily tasks such as cooking or reading or writing

- Listening to one's *mantra* in the mind or in the *anahata chakra*
- Practising the *mantra* with *sumeru* breathing
- Merging the *mantra* into the dot or the *bija* of a given *chakra*, and then observing it emerge from there again
- Taking the *mantra* into the mind's chamber of silence and observing it emerge again from that silence
- Merging the *mantra* into the interior sound in the *bhramara guha* (cave of the bees) and again experiencing its re-emergence
- Using the *mantra* in *manasa-puja* (mental worship) in the interior temples and contemplating on the meaning of one's *mantra*, and unifying that contemplation with *manana*, or the Vedantic contemplation of the *mahavakyas*
- Internal dialogue, a special process of self-purification
- Using the *mantra* as a *bhakti* experience, of devotion and silent prayer, thus merging the path of *bhakti-yoga*, *japa-yoga* and *dhyana-yoga*

There are many other methods of using the *mantra*, which need to be taught by an experienced preceptor who not only teaches the method but also leads the disciple's mind and energies through his own power, that is, he initiates him into the practice.

Shavasana practices serve as ways of entering one's own subtle body. The interior exercises are detailed and complex and go far beyond mere relaxations. They may be practised at the levels of *annamaya kosha*, *pranamaya kosha*, or *manomaya kosha* in a logical progression. The last of these in *shavasana* is *yoga-nidra* at several different levels. For example, one may use it

- to replace sleep

- to heal oneself
- to learn languages
- to effortlessly memorise *sutras* to discover sciences
- to solve problems of philosophical as well as of a personal nature
- to compose instant poetry, or to develop plans
- to master the art of dying
- to enter *samadhi*

For all these, both the method and the initiatory grace are required.

Dharana (concentration) and *pra-vrttis* (resultant experiences): A proficient preceptor in the Himalayan tradition is trained in various methods of concentrations

- on various focal points in the physical body
- at the *chakra* points
- in the *tattvas*, and so forth

The *Vijnana-bhairava tantra* teaches 100 different ways in which an altered state of consciousness may be triggered, and the *Malini-vijayottara-tantra* enumerates nearly 1,300 *dharanas*. And these lists may not be exhaustive. A preceptor trained in the Himalayan tradition needs to know the basic ins and outs of all these concentrations even if he has not practiced them all personally.

Dhyana or meditation proper includes all the methods described above that are integral parts of the approach to meditation, but meditation proper begins at the level of *manomaya kosha*. One may enter that *kosha* in many ways, such as through

- refining the art of *japa*
- subtler steps in breath awareness

- concentration
- initiation
- in the case of a more advanced disciple, a *guru* may simply pull the disciple's mind into a higher degree of meditation. How high one may go through such a conferrment of grace depends on the degree of the preceptor's own advancement. If one has guided the student as far as one has reached, he passes the student on to the higher preceptor

This list of the methods in the Himalayan tradition is only illustrative and is by no means exhaustive.

A qualified preceptor in the Himalayan tradition fulfills at least the following requirements:

- posseses knowledge of the major yoga texts
- practices and been initiated into all the major paths of yoga such as *mantra-yoga, kundalini-yoga, shri-vidya* and so on, with proficiency in some and familiarity with others
- be able to see the association between the Himalayan tradition and other paths, such as those of the Sufis, the Tao, Ch'an, Zen, Theravada, Tibetan, Christian and others, together with their basic texts and historical backgrounds
- be able to assess the personality type to which a given student should be designated so that the student can be
  - led on a complementary path (*bhakti, jnana,* etc.)
  - assigned the proper *mantra,* or *chakra* concentration
  - given progressively appropriate practices
- have at least a certain degree of the power of transmission

Transmission is the central point of the Himalayan tradition. From times immemorial the tradition has been passed on experientially in an unbroken chain of master-disciple relationship. A meditation guide in this tradition must have at least some degree of the power of transmission, to transfer *shakti* to those being taught. He should be able to create a common mind-field when leading a class or a group in meditation and be able to induce a meditative state by his mere presence and voice. One may do so only up to the degree to which he is qualified and authorised. One cannot advise a concentration on, for example, the heart *chakra* unless one can trigger the experience of the energy configurations at least to some degree. Advanced preceptors teach meditation through such a transmission, while using their voices to gently guide their students into a meditative state.

Swami Rama of the Himalayas has presented the Himalayan tradition in its scientific format in his lectures and writings and initiated the disciples to continue a certain degree of transmission.

PART TWO

PRACTICING MEDITATION

CHAPTER 1

WHEN TO MEDITATE?

MEDITATION IN ACTION

Every human being remains dissatisfied if he does not sense progress. In fact all our dissatisfactions arise from our sense of a lack of development in the intangibles of life. The tangibles are only an exterior manifestation. And yet we have somewhere lost touch with the art of enjoying the intangibles. That is what meditation is all about — learning to enjoy the less tangible, the subtle, the fine, and the one closer to the home of our spirit.

Here I wish to draw attention to something that has puzzled me immensely in this life after meeting thousands of people from different countries and different cultures; and I have received quite a few moments of shock. The first shock hit me at the age of twenty-eight, when I came across someone who was not looking for God. I did not know that there were such people too in this world. Lately, the experience of seeing people disturbed has puzzled me, not for lack of empathy but for lack of my own understanding of their situation. People are so dependent on their surroundings. If anything gets disturbed in the surroundings, they feel disturbed. The idea that I am other than my surroundings, that I need not pay attention to disturbances from the surroundings is talked about constantly, but we never quite manage to achieve it or put it into practice.

Some new member of the staff joins me and finds me sitting here with closed eyes. He asks, "Swamiji, shall I switch off the light, or shall I shut your door, or shall I draw the curtains?" I respond, "Whatever for?" And he says, "Oh, so nobody disturbs you!" This idea that in order to meditate the surroundings have to be undisturbed is a very strange one. That, in order for me to be at peace, why should everything around me has to be peaceful? The fact of the matter is that, if I am at peace within myself, then everything around me will automatically and naturally become pacified.

Thus, the disturbances within ourselves generate waves of disturbances around us. People cannot stand crowds. If there are too many people in a room, it is very disturbing. Why is it so? Because the spot where you sit, as I have said many times before, no one else sits there. The space that your body occupies, no one else occupies. People say that we cannot find time to meditate as we are so busy. Sometimes someone has to wait in a car for a few minutes and I tell the person to sit down and use this time. I come out and ask them, "How much *japa* did you do?", I get the reply, "Oh, we are not you, Swamiji. We cannot sit in a car and practice. There are too many thoughts, too many sounds and too many noises and all around are people who want to converse with us." On my part, what I say might seem as a lack of understanding of people's situations. Some people who do not know me, say, "Well Swamiji, it's all right for you to sit in a quiet *ashram* and give us this advice. We have to live out there in the world; what do you know about that?" And I tell them, "I have done half my *sadhana* (meditation) sitting at Canadian and American airports," and they do not believe it.

I would like to suggest that let every year be a year of a very difficult *sadhana* or *sadhana* that you might consider difficult. That is the *sadhana* of meditation in action. Let us get adventurous and do something we've tried occasionally before, but not with full awareness. Meditation while walking alone is easy. One can keep on doing one's *mantra*. But in a crowd? In an office? Waiting outside a shopping mall, sitting in the car? And with the eyes open? Try to practice meditation in action. Let this year be a year wherein by the time Christmas comes and you go for Christmas shopping in the middle of a crowded mall, you find yourself in absolute solitude.

I want you to meditate with your television on; with your walkman on. I want you to meditate while in the arms of your spouse. I want you to meditate with your baby crying in your arms. I want you to meditate waking up, taking a shower or even while cooking a meal. There is no time to especially set aside. When will your *sadhana* be completed? When will we reach our goal? Let there be this longing, the way when you begin to fall in love and day and night, no matter where you are, a certain image of the beloved keeps floating before you. 'The wine of love gets you drunk', as Omar Khayam has said. If we do it as a chore, as an assignment, as a practice, we will not manage it very well. But if at this time, as you read this, there must arise in your heart a longing, an intense longing for that unseen subtle force, by whose very will you are able to hear, whose will is driving me to convey this to you, that is uniting us at these apparently vast distances in a common longing attached to these words. At this very time, let that longing arise in your heart and let that longing not cease.

Let it continue with the same intensity, longing for inner silence.

While having a conversation, go into that part of your mind, which is perpetually silent. You will discover that your voice will change and those around you will begin to experience that silence. Sometimes people will think you are being artificial, but gradually they will accept you and will come to seek your guidance. If you seek the life of meditation in action, many things you do in life as part of your profession, your work, your family life, will become part of your spiritual *sadhana*. For example, at work, many times you have to keep confidences and withhold confidential information. Keeping confidential information is part of the practice of silence. You may say, 'I practice this act of keeping information confidential so I am a great *sadhaka*.' You become a *sadhana* only with the intent, not without the intent. When in your mind you establish the intent that from now on, when I have to keep an information confidential, I shall do it as a part of my spiritual *sadhana* of silence, then it will become a *sadhana*. But if you do it only as part of your job contract, then it ceases to be a *sadhana*. It is the intent that makes it into a *sadhana*.

I have explained the different principles of *sadhana* and their application to regular daily management practices. In the same way, you can take all the different things that you have to do in your business life and find where the intangible principle is. If politeness is merely a business policy, a receptionist speaks politely. Let the receptionist then at the same time earn the merit of *sadhana* by making it into an exercise in egolessness. We cannot be polite without egolessness or without reducing our ego. But the intent is what makes it a *sadhana*. If it is only a part of our training in communication; then it is not a *sadhana*. Our training in gentle communication becomes a part of our intent to practice *ahimsa* (non-violence), before becoming a *sadhana*. Take any of the principles that you use in your business, in your family life, in the contractual area of social connections, and try to examine where they fit as part of the spiritual life. This way, you will enhance your practice of meditation in action.

If you have a doubt as to how to make your regular daily business practices into a *sadhana*, and you're not sure where it connects with your spiritual life, I don't mind receiving a brief e-mail from you and I will try and answer it to the best of my ability. For now, just begin. Begin to look at all the things you have to do that are right business practices and see to which principle of *yamas* and *niyamas*, *karma* and so on, they are related. Shift your intent and you will not find a conflict between your daily life and your spiritual life. Soon other things will happen. You will experience a sense of satisfaction that you have not experienced before. And along with that sense of satisfaction and a certain peace of mind, you will find that your meditation itself develops at the same time as your exterior worldly life becomes successful.

Along with this aspect of meditation in action, try reading the perennial philosophy of the *Bhagavad Gita*, and learn how not to be affected by your surroundings. Try practicing meditation in crowded, noisy places. Gradually you will develop the ability to calm the minds of those who become agitated in the presence of the causes of agitation.

A young man at my *ashram* told me of a boy, who can neither hear nor speak nor see, yet he has taught him meditation. I asked him, how and he said, "I touch his throat to make him realise that I am referring to his breathing, then I gently bring my hand down to his stomach and diaphragm, give it a very gentle push and release till he begins to feel it. And the young man says, 'I speak into his mind' and he understands. If he does not see me every week, he pleads with his mother to bring him to me, because he enjoys the experience so much." A boy who cannot hear, who cannot speak, who cannot see, has been taught meditation.

We do not know how fortunate we are to be granted this gift of life. Do not lose this opportunity as life passes day by day, month by month, year by year. Let the longing for complete peace become intense in your heart and then in everything that you do — you will find a connection with the principles of *sadhana*. If you try to cut down on your food intake only to lose weight, you will long for that food because you have not found the inner satisfaction. But when you make it a part of the *sadhana* of fasting for spiritual reasons, then you will succeed. And this rings true in all your pursuits. Establish these connections. Don't do things only for their exterior, utilitarian value. The whole civilisation will change. The very texture of business relations will change. And non-violence will become a part of your contractual theory. In other words, where it is merely a contract not to hurt each other, it will become a *sadhana* as we shall proceed into making ourselves the kind of saintly beings on whose lap the tiger rests his head on one side, and on the other side a fawn rests his head and both are caressed equally. But before we graduate to the tiger and the fawn, let us start with the neighbour and the spouse; with the quarrelling siblings. Let us analyse a situation which exemplifies how our behaviour enables us to resolve a conflict: two persons are fighting, quarrelling on the streets. A policeman intervenes as part of his duty because he has to maintain law and order. I pass by and I just look at one of these quarrelling persons in the eye and smile. He smiles back, in most cases. Then I do the same with the other party and then I walk on. Because to me the *sadhana* part is more effective than trying to keep law and order on the streets. It becomes a practice of spirituality, of *ahimsa* (non-violence). Learn to reinterpret, reconnect things that have become disconnected from spiritual principles, but are very much present. Reconnect and you will not have a conflict between daily life and spirituality. Let your life be of integration and I look forward to hearing that you have resolved the conflict between life and spirituality.

CHAPTER 2

THE SEAT OF MEDITATION

From time to time thoughts awaken from the writings that have been preserved in the great ancient texts, the thoughts that came to the minds of the ancient masters, recorded in the scriptures and handed down for thousands of years.

Sometimes when I read these ancient traditions and scriptures, I get ecstatic and cannot help wanting to share those words with you also, as well as my own thoughts that are inspired by them.

The thoughts expressed here concern a meditation hut. There is a portable meditation hut that I have been living in for the last sixty-four years. It is travelling around with me and I travel in it. It is a hut; it is a chariot; some call it a body. But then if I was not so body-bound, I would like to have a different kind of meditation hut. That is the kind that I describe in the following words. These words were originally written in the Hindi language and languages, says the great poet Rabindranath Tagore, are jealous. You cannot really translate. An Italian proverb says that to translate is to betray. Some of the words, idioms, proverbs or associations cannot be expressed in another language; they do not sound the same. They neither carry the force nor do they convey the sentiment. Still, I shall try to do my very best to translate.

I have built myself a meditation hut.

I have built a meditation hut for myself, far from the traffic of planets and their satellites, where even thoughts from the minds of the dwellers of various worlds cannot reach me. At a curve of the vast space beyond, where three space-flowing energy-rivers converge, there, in a place called *tri-kuti prayaga*, I have built myself a meditation hut. In the traditions of India, whenever three rivers meet, it is considered a sacred spot. At certain times, millions of people gather together to pray and immerse themselves in the river waters for a sacred bath. Many of the famous places where two or three rivers meet are called *prayagas*. It means a place of intensively performed sacraments, because in ancient times the great *rishis* sat in *ashrams* and forests of these areas to perform lengthy and intensive fire-offerings and other sacred acts.

Tri-kuti is a triangular centre in the upper half of the forehead, so I have named this place *tri-kuti prayaga*. Here it is suggested to read a book entitled *From Sea to Sky* by Edmund Hillary, the conqueror of Mount Everest. It is the description of a journey up the River Ganges, but not merely that, it is one that speaks of the Gangetic culture, the culture of the people on both sides of the river. One of the places he passes through is Prayaga, the modern city of Allahabad, just west of Varanasi in the plains. Then, after a thousand miles or perhaps more, he comes to a place called Devaprayaga, where two tributaries of the river meet, and from that place south, the river is called the Ganges. Similarly, further up the mountains are Nandaprayaga and Rudraprayaga and so on. In the composition presented here, we have a *tri-kuti prayaga*, a meeting place of three rivers in a triangular spot in the upper half of the forehead, where three *kundalini* rivers have their confluence. You may build your meditation hut here.

To ward off the invasions of intruding thoughts of the world-dwellers, I have done many *dig-bandhanas* by reciting *bhur, bhuvah, svah,* several times. I have preserved these *dig-bandhanas.* Many meditators are familiar with the word *dig-bandhana* (tying-up the directions, tying-up the ten quarters around you). After sitting down for meditation, if you want to do it externally, sprinkling a stream of water around you, or (internally) visualise three circles of light around you. This is done with the mental recitation of the *mantra: Om, bhur, bhuvah, svah,* which is the first addendum to the Gayatri *mantra.*

Before one begins meditation, the first act one may perform is this *dig-bandhana,* to ward off all intruding thoughts. I have erected the walls of my meditation hut. They are very firm!

On the surfaces of an unaccountable number of earths, the sheets of sunshine and moonlights lie strewn about. They're indeed very light: whoever needs, may carry them away. I have picked up many from several earths, and made of them the roof and the ceiling of my hut. It's really very attractive!

On the lily petals, in so many dewdrops, are imprisoned such beautiful rainbows. The dew dries up, the rainbows imprisoned therein wilt away and are extinguished. I went around to gather these dewdrops. By casting my affection-filled glances upon them, I opened their doors, and the rainbows, thus released, sprang to freedom and now form the arches for my meditation hut. They're really very charming.

The souls who become liberated after attaining the highest *samadhi* are like a novice renunciate, who sheds the clothing he wore as a householder; and after renouncing, never looks back again. So do the liberated souls drop their subtle bodies and senses by the wayside and never care for them again. I have gathered those subtle body senses and made from them the doors and windows of my meditation hut, and I have hung on them curtains made of the pearls that the world knows as inspirational revelations but that, truly drop from the necklace of Mother Sharada, when the music of her playing the *veena*, reaches them; and its ripples vibrate and pluck them. The pearls that the swans of Mother Saraswati were unable to pick in their beaks plentiful around the lake of Manasa. Of the senses of the subtle body, one needs to study the lectures on the gross body, the subtle body, the causal body, and the seventeen constituents of the subtle body. Two words for the great Mother of the Universe: Sharada and Saraswati, the lady of wisdom, music, knowledge, and inspiration. White clad, with a swan for her vehicle, carrying a *veena*, a most ancient and powerful stringed musical instrument on which the Vedic hymns were, and are still sung. When the musicians of India train, they sit before the icon of Saraswati (also known as Sharada) at the hour of God in the morning, and dedicate their music as a prayer-offering to her. The dancers too train by offering their dance as a homage to her. One of the most sacred and difficult pilgrimages is to Mount Kailash, which is the northernmost home of Shiva, where he, the Lord of meditators, sits, though the processions of history may come and go. It is a mountain in Tibet, now under Chinese occupation. A few pilgrims still visit and circumambulate this mountain at the height of 18,000 feet or so. At the foot of the mountain is a lake, known as Lake Manasa. It simply means 'the mind'. The allusion here is to the mental image that the great Mother drops many of her pearls in the Lake of the Mind, and those that her swans do not pick in their beaks are left strewn around, for devotees like us to pick and to make curtains from; beading them through breath strings and hanging these beaded strings on the curtains of the senses. Thus you shall have the doors and windows of the senses curtained. I filled my hands many times over, to bead them to make my curtains.

At the hour of God before Usha, the deity of dawn, appears with the red cinnabar dot of the sun upon her forehead, I go to take my sacred morning immersion at the convergence of those space-flowing rivers. In the vessel made of the silver of rays, I bring holy water from the milk-river of the galaxy — drinking which, the Lord of creation, the Lord of preservation and the Lord of destruction have been satiating themselves for cycles upon cycles of creation. How much more so of a mortal's mind? Only a few drops, touched upon the limbs of a mortal's mind, cause all thirst, hunger and craving to dissipate and disappear.

The hour of God is a measure of time called *brahma-muhurta*. As the night is divided into four sections, in the ancient *ashrams* and among those very few who still carry on the tradition, the first quarter of the night is spent in meditation. The second and third quarters of the night are meant for sleeping. And the fourth quarter of the night, from 3:00 a.m. to 6:00 a.m. is the hour of *amrita*, the hour when the elixir of immortality, the drink of the gods, drops from the heaven on the crown of the head. Listen to the sound of silence at that hour. Drink the cup of solitude at that hour until the music that rises within your heart and mind merges with the music that the birds make. And then arise from your meditation seat. You will need no other wine.

Usha, the ancient Vedic name for dawn may represent the

dawning of wisdom before full daybreak, that is enlightenment. 'The red-cinnabar dot of the sun' represents the dot of fortune, which the married women of India wear at the spot of the third eye, above the centre, between the eyebrows. The chemical name for cinnabar is mercuric sulphide, representing the philosophy of alchemy, i.e. the total balance of the universal male (mercury) and the universal female (sulphur). In the traditions of yoga, the sun is the name of the universal spiritual energy, as taught and awakened in the solar science.

The Sanskrit word for Milky Way is *Akasha Ganga*, the Ganges of Space. The suggestions of the Milky Way and the Gangetic holiness are combined here in 'milk-river'. It is said in India's cosmology that the Lord or the preserver sleeps on the coiled up serpent of infinity on the ocean of light (milk), after the universe is dissolved and before the next universe emanates.

When the gods, the shining ones, come bathing at the convergence of these rivers, they splash many a star. These sprinklings sometimes come through the windows into my meditation hut. I gather them and I tie them in a neat bundle. They serve me through the night like little gems, casting their glow and providing me with illumination. They last with me for a very long time.

Ah, yes, the three flaws of *Prakriti*, Mother Nature, which are known as the three *gunas* (qualities), sometimes cast a shadow, like clouds, over the roof of my hut. I immediately sprinkle the *mantra*-consecrated waters upon it and wash the spots away, lest they accumulate and form for me another mortal, physical body.

Prakriti or *Prakrti* in *Samkhya* philosophy is what might be translated as the origin of Nature, the origin of the material universe, a state in which the *gunas* (*sattva*, *rajas*, and *tamas*), the three-fold forces of the universe, the three powers, the three attributes, in equilibrium, are in absolute balance. Then *rajas*, the agitating force, disturbs the equilibrium, and out of a pin-point of light, burst the galaxies. Later they return to the same. In philosophy there are three attributes or three forces. In the Sanskrit language and in Hindi, the word *guna* also means 'good quality', and I have also called them her flaws (actually the English word 'good' is derived from the word *guna*, or is cognate to this word). They cast their shadow upon my meditation hut, and I sprinkle the *mantra*-consecrated water from my vessel, made of rays of silver, to wash off the spots, lest they gather and gather, and become thicker and thicker; so that the shadows become spots, and the spots become new bodies to reincarnate me into this physical world again.

The solitude here is such that only a soul in a cognitive *samadhi* can experience. As I said, no mind of any dweller of the three words can come here and intrude into my solitude. A cognitive, *a-samprajnata samadhi*, the highest state of consciousness in which the spirit knows itself, unalloyed with matter.

Three words: *bhur, bhuvah, svah* — earth, sky and heavens — signify first, being up to the third *chakra* in the navel region, second up to the fifth *chakra* in the throat, and the third one above these. But, yes, it did so happen once: I was submerged into the ocean of the joy and bliss of deep meditation, like the reflection of a full moon immersed in a ripple-free, absolutely still, crystalline, clear lake, yet the sound of a song — sung in a feminine voice — sweet, yet filled with pathos, reached me. She was a Brahmani, the lady consort of Brahma — the lord of universe, which existed in a rock on the side of a mountain upon a distant earth.

The spirit whose body is a universe is called Brahma; his feminine consort is Brahmani. Just as common mortals view the frame of their flesh to be themselves, so may a universal being identify with the universe-body. None of these are transcendent or highest spiritual stations.

When my eyes and ears came into the half-awake state, out of meditation, she addressed me: "For countless aeons, my dear Lord, my husband, has been performing his intense, ascetic endeavours to obtain liberation. Neither does he become liberated, nor do I receive the marital joy and bliss that is the share of a dedicated consort. My internal life has been filled with agitation, and through that, not only the living beings of my universe, but also the forests, trees, vines, grains, plants, suns, moons, rivers, lakes, oceans of all my worlds have become agitated, as though passing through a volcanic quake. I fear what destruction might be waiting around the corner of time! Is our universe going to be dissolved, without my Lord, my husband, ever gaining his liberation?"

How could I not, hearing such a plea, melt with compassion? The passage of time in the rock-universes is immensely slow. The equivalent of one day for human beings becomes a thousand years in the rock-universes. If I had made no attempt to free the Brahma and the Brahmani, the Lord and the Lady of that universe, from the travails and tortures, lasting such a long period, would not the dwellers of that universe scorch themselves in all the three kinds of heat of suffering, and would they not have created a hell for themselves in their world? Then, knowing myself to be responsible for such devastation, would I have been able to sit in my solitude and enjoy my meditation without any distractions arising out of the memory of a duty not yet discharged?

The three *tapas* (pronounced *taapas*) are three kinds of heat or burning. Not the good kind of burning known as *tapas* (pronounced with short a's), ascetic perseverance, which is the ascetic heat to burn impurities, but the three *tapas* (*taapas*), by which we ourselves burn: the mental ones, the physical ones, and the ones that exist in our surroundings, in our societies in the world, in Nature and in the environment. When our interior *tapas* (*taapas*) gather their force together and converge, they become the fires of hell. Then truly a hell is created in a given universe.

So I went to that Lady's world with her. It must have taken us at least as much time as passes in a hundred-millionth part of a micro moment. Then the problem arose: on the one hand, I, a brilliant, minute photon of light, and on the other, that rock-solid universe — how was I to enter it?

By the power of my intentness, with the force of my *sankalpa* (resolve), all of it that I could muster, applying the entire force of the concentrations that I had learned, I managed to break through that solid state and, making the outer surface of the rock somewhat thus transparent, I entered into the universe within it.

According to the *Yoga Vasishtha* text, the universe, that is our experience of it, is nothing but a projection of the spirit's resolve to ideate, to emanate, as an idea in a given form. The more intense this *sankalpa*, the more 'solid' is the appearance of realities.

Brahma, the Lord of that universe, using a pebble-world for his meditation seat, was indeed making a God-like effort to go deeper and deeper into meditation, but, because of so many affairs of that universe that must pass through his mind, there was no end to the distractions disturbing his self-contemplation. The worlds are but pebbles flying about as and in mind-time-space-causation coordinates.

As many as 18,000 cycles of creation and dissolution have already passed. Half of that Brahma's life span have already been spent, and after another 18,000 cycles of creation and dissolution, the final mega-dissolution of that universe would occur, and along with it, he too would die.

This life-span is normally 100 years only; each cycle of creation and dissolution of the cosmos is counted as one day; thus 100 years mean 36,000 cycles of creation and dissolution.

There may be innumerable minor creations and dissolutions of little universes in a cosmos at any given time. A mega-dissolution, *maha-pralaya*, is the dissolution of an entire cosmos.

With this *abhinivesha*, he was fear-stricken. I gave him the *diksha*, the initiation of bursting through the highest point of the Brahma-opening in the skull and returned to my meditation hut, and the time that still remained of that micro moment, I utilised in the joy of unbreakable intentness.

Since then, would you like to know what I have done? There were still some *dig-bandhanas* left over after I had made the walls of my hut. With a few more *dig-bandhanas* added, I constructed a fence around my cottage. Now, even the stream of distractions from the minds of the Brahmas and the Brahmanis of any universe, no matter how sharp, no matter how forceful they might be, can pierce through these fences to intrude into the secret mystery of the seat of my consciousness. Only my *gurudeva*, Acharya Hiranyagarbha whose name means the 'master of the golden womb', whose cottage is quite distant from here, on the mountain peak of Chidakasha, the peak of the mountain known as the 'sky of consciousness', when he considers me deserving, unasked, when I am least expecting it, finally casts a ray of his light towards me. And that light, passing through the fences and the walls of my hut, pierces through my *Brahma-bindu,* the point of Brahman in the skull.

Hiranya-garbha, the golden womb, is the name given by *yogis* to the first *guru* who is the spirit as the teacher, whose embodiment are the personal teachers. *Acharya* means a master who teaches.

Bindu is the point, from which the universe emanates and into which it dissolves. In *samadhi* it is an experience of the point that is God, *Brahma-bindu,* located in the centre of the thousand-petal lotus in the skull.

This ray of light, sent from the mountain peak of the 'sky of consciousness', frees me, liberates me, burning those lily petals along with the letters written upon them, from *a* to *ham,* from alpha to omega, of which I have at any time claimed proprietorship, any of which I have identified myself with. It makes me truly the son of the goddess who is known as Aparna, the leafless one, she, who when performing her ascetic endeavours to be united with her Lord Shiva, fasted. First she abandoned grains. Then she abandoned fruits. Then she lived on leaves and lily petals. And then, having consumed them, she was Sushumna, the slim, brilliant lady, having lost all worldly right, a straight sword of lightning passing through the spine, but without any leaves or petals and only reaching a single point from which the universes are created and into which the universes dissolve. I truly become her son.

In the letters written on the lotus petals from *a* to *ham,* the word *a-ham* means 'I' in Sanskrit. That is what we have in *so-ham*. *So* means 'that'. *Aham* means 'I am'. A is the first letter of the Sanskrit alphabet, and *ha* is the last letter. A letter becomes a *mantra* through nasalisation as in *ham*. In the vibratory principle, the different petals of the lotuses of the *chakras* are inscribed, as it were, with the specific letters assigned to them. All of the vibratory forces put together, expressed in these letters of the alphabet, *a* to *ham*, constitute *aham*: the 'I' with which you identify, the 'I' on which you have a claim of proprietorship.

Based on the story of Parvati, the eternal consort of Shiva, in *kundalini-yoga*, when *sushumna*, the central stream of divine consciousness and life force, is re-united with the Lord as *Brahma-bindu*, there are no more emanations of centripetal and centrifugal forces forming petals in the whirling wheels of *chakras*.

Whosoever is weary, whosoever is scorched with thirst, whosoever feels broken by the slaps of craving, whosoever the dualities and the principles of opposites have torn into shreds, let him seek this balm of solitude. Let him take to this meditation as his potion, prescription and provender for the path.

Dig-bandhanas can be performed in a moment. There is no shortage of the sheets of sunshine and moonlights strewn about. In the Forest of Lilies, the dewdrops are an uncountable million, the rainbows imprisoned in them longing to be released, relieved, to be allowed to bloom and open up. From the great Mother's necklace, the pearls drop like dots of snow from the snow-laden trees when a few gusts of wind touch them.

The *pranas* are the animating forces that emanate from the mind and move the physical forces of the body.

The one who desires can find one of the confluences of space-rivers, for there are innumerable such convergences. Let him make a cottage at his own *trikuti-prayaga,* fill his vessel made of the silver of rays daily with waters of the milky river of the galaxy, touch it to his limbs and be free of hunger, thirst and craving. Drunk on the wine of solitude, let him in the same way live the life of joy and carefree pleasure, as I do since I have built myself a meditation hut.

This writing is inspired from the great text, the *Yoga-Vasistha* — an epic in 26,000 verses of lyrical, philosophical poetry, rare in world literature.

CHAPTER 3

FEELINGS WHILE MEDITATING

The time we spend in meditation is very precious. As we lead a busy life, these few minutes that we have should be utilised with diligence. During that time, we must forget the world, our conflicts, our unfulfilled desires and our deep-rooted emotional splits. There are only two occasions in our life which are worthwhile — the one in which we help someone, serve someone selflessly and the other we spend calming our mind and preparing for God. Everything else is given to a means, as a tool, to support these two occasions. We end up spending twenty-three hours and fifty-five minutes in support systems and for the actual pursuit of meditation we have only five minutes left and even those five minutes are encroached upon. So, by the time we finish those five minutes, we have actually meditated perhaps only for thirty seconds or maybe for a minute or two minutes. This is insufficient. Therefore, these few minutes should be guarded with great care.

Talking of distractions during meditation (the first distraction are verbal thoughts), all the arguments that go on in the mind against ourselves, against somebody else, against somebody who isn't doing right to us and so on and so forth are included.

Sometimes attacks even against the present learned master arise: "Why hasn't he replied? These teachers don't really care; they just come once in a while, do their job and go away. You can't really depend on them when you really need them. I was told meditation would lead me to such peace that it will solve all my problems. What good is it? Why do I have to sit? They have funny ways of shutting us up when we ask questions." All such conflicts go on constantly in the mind.

When somehow we manage to calm ourself through positive counter-arguments or just saying, 'Okay, never mind, I have these twenty-five minutes not of total peace, but relative peace. At least for these twenty-five minutes my husband will leave me alone, if he will. Or my kids. It is a good excuse to have a moment to myself and be quiet. Alright, I won't let these thoughts intrude on my breath, my *mantra*. Hey, I'm not sitting straight anymore.' So you straighten yourself. Then, after a while, visual images start emerging. Those visual images have some connection with the thoughts you were thinking but they are very remote. They arise from the world of *samskaras* or from the imprints that you have left on your mind. They arrive seemingly out of the blue and there is no apparent logic as to why a given image arises at that moment. You weren't thinking about it. It had no connection (apparent connection) with the previous thought you had been thinking and suddenly there it is — you know — on some street in Los Angeles. You never thought of the scene, and suddenly you are catching a bus to meet somebody and then there the thoughts go again. The world of *samskaras*, the hidden imprints in our unconscious, have a dynamics of their own. They are not something dead sitting in a record in a book, which until we open the book keep on just sitting there. In fact, it is more like the sub-surface activity of the ocean.

Our unconscious mind is like the ocean with a tremendous amount of sub-surface activity of the conscious mind; the surface activity can never come anywhere near in comparison. The activity in the sub-surface unconscious mind determines our direction unless we overcome it by a conscious will and conscious decision — our freedom of will (which we possess). What we do with our conscious mind has no bearing on these thoughts of the unconscious mind. This is because the conscious thoughts we think are only of those moments of our life which we consciously remember. The next week we won't remember in which corner of this room we were sitting and at what angle we were looking at the light or at the speaker. But our unconscious mind will remember that. 'Remember that' means to have the imprint or a complete picture. And it has a complete picture of millions of lifetimes. And there's constant agitation, constant movement, going on in that ocean of our unconscious.

A single wave on the surface of the ocean arises from God knows how many different powers combined — the motion of the Earth on its axis (rotation), the motion of the Earth in the orbit around the sun (revolution), the gravitational pull of the sun, the gravitational pull of the moon, constant meteoric showers, the volcanic eruptions at the bottom of the sea, the movement of the tectonic plates, the sound waves that go on underneath the ocean, all the different channels where the rain is falling, where the rain has not fallen enough, the melting of snow-caps and so on. How many different forces combine to produce that one single *vritti* (propensity) of the mind?

With all this tremendous action going on underneath the surface, which wave will arise at any given time cannot be determined. Where this wave will appear you cannot determine.

Quite often there is no logical reason why a certain visual image arises in your meditation. But it is a disturbance. If you continue to pursue it, it rejoices. I caught him! Trapped him. I can drag him down into the depths of the unconscious mind. So the moment the thought of the visual image arises, the answer is indifference or ignorance. When a dog jumps at you, the ideal situation would be to stay calm. The more you react or get back, the more excited it gets and jumps. The only way to stop the dog from pouncing at you is to cross your arms and become totally and mentally indifferent. Then it goes and sits down in a corner. The answer to these kinds of unnecessary random thoughts is simply that you cannot get involved in them. When you have somehow managed to learn to ignore them, then the third stage arises interspersed by these other two intrusions I have talked about — intrusion of thoughts and intrusion of visual images.

This third feeling comprises vague sentiments which could be of joy and ecstasy sometimes, or sadness, or sometimes what people mistake to be sexual arousal in meditation. Actually these are fears of one kind or another. Sometimes it is an actual fear; sometimes just a hesitation. It is like the hesitation one feels when one dives into the water. At a certain depth, one wants to come up. One has the capacity to go further, but doubts whether to go on or not. It is this quick and momentary feeling — either you succumb to it and you come up or you can ignore the feeling and go to your full length. This kind of hesitation about going into the depths of meditation, which also becomes a fear at times, is again a trick played by your unconscious mind. There is nothing to be afraid of. There is no cause out there or in there or wherever it is. It is your own unconscious link to other fears. That is why the Buddhist philosophers always say, 'virya', strength. Or the

Upanishads say, "Nyamatma balanhin enalabhya" — the self is not to be found by a weakling.

If you succumb to fear, you will always be afraid and end up becoming a weakling. Today you are afraid of a little thing, tomorrow you will be afraid of something more and you will build yourself fortresses upon fortresses of protective layering. One wall more and that will protect you, you think. But it won't. Hence, this is my formula about fear: if I am afraid of something, I give myself the freedom to be afraid, but I don't give myself the freedom to run away from the object of fear. You can tremble all you want, but go right to the source of the fear and face it.

If I hesitate to do something, I think, 'Why am I hesitating? Is there a rational reason for just a fear?' Examine the source of those fears. If it is just a fear, I can postpone dealing with it for a while; that will be alright. I can wait, but you know that you have to eventually deal with it by looking it in the eye. Just do it. That's my way.

My master's way is, "Don't postpone. Do it now." I haven't reached there yet. Keep up your meditation practice if you do nothing else.

Just go and do it. I am not saying, "Don't hesitate on the way", that is natural, but "Go, do it!" and you discover that the task is done. Get through with it and get there. Halfway there you might panic; that's fine. You have the freedom to panic. If you see a ghost walking in the night, go towards it, get close and take a good look. You will be the only one in the world who has actually seen a ghost face-to-face and you can come back and tell everybody about your experience.

PART THREE

PERSONA OF A MEDITATOR

YOGI'S SCHEDULE

RECOMMENDED DISCIPLINES OF THE DAY

It is quite difficult to discipline oneself. I myself don't even like the word. If somewhere the word discipline is written, I run from that room. After having taught for almost thirty-six years of my life, I have never ever practiced discipline. Believe it or not, I do absolutely whatever I feel inclined to do. That is my happiness. The only thing I have done is to train my inclinations. When you were a child of three or four, your mother must have been a harsh disciplinarian, meaning she always wanted you to brush your teeth. And what a chore that was to brush your teeth every day! But as an adult, you don't have a mother on your head, pushing you and coaxing you to brush your teeth. You are completely free. Try not to brush your teeth for a week. It has become a discipline. What is a discipline in the beginning gradually becomes a habit. You cannot do without it any more. It becomes natural and gets ingrained in the mind. What one does need to do is to train one's inclinations. How does one train one's inclinations? Simply by training one's thought or by making a quiet resolve in the mind: 'This is the way I would like to be. This is the direction I would like to take. That is what I would like my day to be like. I know this is mentally healthy, physically healthy.' And if you do not succeed the first time, you have committed no sin. Whatever is in yoga is recommended. No one stands over you with a stick. No one says, 'Thou shalt do so, thou shalt not do so or otherwise you will go to hell.' There is no such requirement. Another corollary of training one's inclinations towards success in practicing a discipline is the absence of guilt.

NO GUILT, RATHER JUST TRY AGAIN

The word 'guilt' is a very strange word. People have great difficulty with guilt. I have great difficulty with the word guilt. I have not yet understood what people mean by this word. I know it is a great social crime to make somebody feel guilty. And I am guilty of that crime at times. I am told, "You make me feel guilty." And I am flabbergasted. What did I do? What do you mean by guilty? Feel guilty? I really have not understood the word because in my own upbringing, training, or spiritual and cultural background, the word never arose. Some day I may understand the word.

You drive a car on the freeway and the brakes do not work. What do you do? You pull over to one side and stop the ignition. You don't put your head on the steering wheel and feel guilty. You don't sit there and say, 'My God, I didn't take care of these brakes before, I feel so guilty. I'll never be able to drive again.' Or if a tyre gets punctured, what do you do? Do you sit there and feel guilty? Something is missing in your vehicle or you have neglected to take care of, so you get out of the car and call for help. You get the screw fixed, you get the brakes taken care of and you drive off and go on. What is this 'guilt' business? To me guilt is a very positive word. It is simply the recognition of the fact that I didn't quite make it this time. And from that I would like to continue trying. That alone should be the meaning of guilt. Thus, if you do not quite manage to train your inclinations to the point where you would like to maintain the discipline of the day, that is fine. When your hour for introspection at night comes, you recognise that the day didn't go too well. Relax about it, go into your *shavasana*, watch your breath, go to sleep. And that marks the start of your next day.

TO START YOUR DAY, BEGIN AS YOU WENT TO BED THE PREVIOUS NIGHT

We have a saying in the yoga tradition that whatever is the sum total of a person's thoughts throughout his life, that sum total will concern him at the hour of death. And that sum total that comes flashing in front of his eyes at the hour of death is what determines his next life in reincarnation. The same applies to our shorter cycle of the day and night. This life is an unbroken sentence from the moment we were like a tiny jellyfish stuck to the mother's uterus. Whatever bare essentials of a feeling of awareness began, they have continued unbroken. With whatever thoughts you fall asleep at night, you will find that with that very thought you wake up the next morning. With whatever mood you go to bed at night, the same mood continues the next morning. Your first thought of the day, your first mood of the morning, determines the momentum for almost your entire day. And in order to have a good day, the whole day, have a good morning, have a good night and to have a good night, have a good thought before falling asleep.

a) Go to sleep in a good mood

Reading something inspiring or beautiful creates a good mood. Read the biographies of great saints; read the lives of great *yogis* of the East or the West. See how others have solved their life problems. See how they have emerged out of a period of darkness.

No matter how busy you are, no matter how distressed you are, keep a book by your bedside and read half a page, one page or even three lines — it will change your mood; it will comfort you. It will give you solace. You can say, 'I have read it all before. I know all about it,' but you have seen the same shops before and you keep looking at them. You have seen your husband before, you keep looking at him. You have seen your wife before, and you keep looking at her; you've seen your children before, but you keep looking at them. Just as you are adding all of these *samskaras*, all of these fine subtle impressions in your mind, keep reinforcing these highly constructive, inspiring *samskaras*, to your mind over and over again because they become part of the sum total of your mind. And over a period of time they will give you momentum and a direction. You train your inclinations each time they help you to reaffirm your resolve to seek blessings, to seek perfection, to seek the bliss of liberation, to help others to be unselfish. One of the books that is highly recommended is the *Bhagavad Gita* — 'The Song of the Lord'. There are many translations available. It is the world's only scripture that deals with life. It was taught in the middle of the battlefield. Two armies are standing and Krishna teaches Arjuna (one of the five Pandava brothers) while the armies are waiting. It deals with the battlefield of life. It dwells on having the virtue of action without the desire for fruit — actions surrendered to the Lord; actions without attachment. Another great book I know of is called *Woods of God Realisation*. This is a three-or four-volume work by Swami Rama Tirtha, who was a *swami* of great spiritual accomplishments and a highly moving and inspiring personality. He lived in the United States around early 1900 and this book, *Woods of God Realisation*, consists of his lectures given for those three or four years in California at that time. You can open the book anywhere and be inspired. Another book I recommend strongly is *Living with the Himalayan Masters*.

b) Before going to sleep, spend a little time to introspect

Did I maintain mindfulness during the day today? Did I manage it? What is it I did not manage? How would I like to manage it tomorrow? How would I like to be a better person tomorrow than I have been today? Where is it that I failed? Where is it that my emotion overcame my discrimination and judgement?

This may take the form of writing a spiritual diary. Going over the pages of the diary every now and then enables to set yourself on a spiritual project. You work with yourself and constantly watch. Write that diary, if not on paper, then in your mind and reaffirm your resolve. And then go to sleep with a short relaxation and with the awareness of your breathing, have a good night's rest.

c) Go to sleep completely relaxed

Find release in *shavasana* (the corpse posture), with awareness of your breathing. Centralise your thoughts; have a centred personality. When you wake up in the morning, you will wake up refreshed and energised.

HOW TO BEGIN YOUR DAY?

a) Begin the day by getting in touch with yourself

When I was a child under training by my father, I was taught to keep a tiny little mirror under my pillow at night and first thing in the morning, open my eyes and look at my face. That was the first form of concentration I was taught when I was little. From the age of four-and a-half to about seven or eight, I had that concentration. First thing in the morning, look at your face. And for another concentration, look at the face in the mirror, put the mirror aside and maintain the face. I can still see that face. We have a saying in India — sometimes if your day is not going too well, we say, 'Who's face did you see first thing in the morning?' Because whichever face you see, the mood of that face also hits you if you are sensitive, and you are sensitive at that hour of the morning. You are very receptive at that hour of the morning. Begin your day with getting in touch with yourself. The foundation for the day should be firm. I would not say, sleep with a mirror under your pillow, but remember the principle that the state of consciousness should be changed very gently. We are taught that when we have to wake someone, gently rub the toes; start at the extreme distance from the brain, from the mind. Then rub the hands and reach towards the forehead gently and lovingly. You want to wake a child, or your wife, husband, friend, then start very gently, very affectionately. Consciousness comes gently and the person wakes with a mood of feeling loved. Don't go into the room, bang the door, and scream, "Hey, wake up!" Also when someone is meditating, go very gently. People who are in deep meditation, sometimes can be jarred badly. And sometimes, great masters who walk into God consciousness are often not even aware of the body, even when they are talking. I know an instance that took place when Shivanat, my friend who is in Minneapolis, who served Swami Rama as a young boy when *swamiji* was practicing in the cave in the Himalayas. *Swamiji* was talking and Shivanat touched him, and he said, "Don't you ever do that. You'll kill me." Because you would think that their consciousness is with you, but only one sense is with you. The rest is in their own world. Try to use your internal alarm clock and if you have gone to sleep with a relaxed mind, that clock will wake you up.

b) Once awake, do not lie there tossing and turning

"In a moment, I'll get up." Five minutes stretch to two hours. "Oh, my I missed my meditation time!" It is very difficult for a mother, parents with children and others, to maintain that mood, but try. Wake up in the morning and do not lie there fantasising, because this way you set the fantasy for the day. It will linger for the whole day and affect your mindfulness. As soon as you wake up, sit up and the way you open your eyes from meditation to your palms, open your eyes to your palms. Your most prominent cognitive sense, your eyes, touches your most prominent active sense — the hand and the whole process of cognition and action, of stimulus and response, beigins with establishment of your own circuit. We have a saying in India that all the gods dwell in our two hands. May God bless those who have hands. We have another saying that the Goddess of wealth lives in the fingertips, the Goddess of learning in the middle of the hand and God himself dwells at the base of the palm. You can take it literally or figuratively; your hands are sacred. They are your means of support, your way of action, your means of performing *karma* (action) in life. Get in touch with your hands. Look at your hands as though reading from left to right, or from top to bottom. Centre yourself and then say a prayer; join your hands before the heart and bow your head. In India this is also the normal greeting to people — *namaste*. When you meet people, you fold your hands before the heart, bow your head, signifying that 'with all the love of the heart, with all the power of action in my hands, with all the power of my head, I love you, I honour and worship the deity who lives in you.' At the *ashram* in Minneapolis, in Honesdale and in other *ashrams*, we recite some verses mentally or together at that moment, reaffirming our divine nature. The first verse of the series runs:

Pratah smarami hrdi samsphura datma-tattvam
sac-cit-sukham parama-hansa gatim turiyam.
Yat-svapna-jagrat-suspti mavaiti nityam
tad Brahma niskala maham na ca bhuta-sanghah.

At dawn do I meditate on that which shines in the heart as the self, the truth; that which is existence-intelligence-happiness; that which is the goal of the great sages; that which is the transcendent reality. I am that eternal Brahman who is unblemished and which knows the three states of dream — waking and sleep and not the aggregate of elements.

Having reaffirmed that divine nature, having started with positive thoughts, put your foot down from the bed with a happy mind, because even as the *Bible* says, you are made in the image of the divine being. You walk like a God of earth; not repressed, not depressed, but joyful and happy. When you are in possession of that inner joy, even when penniless, you walk like an emperor.

c) The physical area of our day

One of the habits that I find missing in the present civilisation is the habit of a fixed time for the bowel movement. The first thing in all non-Western cultures is that people have a bowel movement at a designated time. They have been trained to do that from childhood. It's performed first thing in the morning. You cannot sit down and carry on with breathing exercises and meditation and so on while your system inside is not quite clean. At a later age in life, the habit is difficult to form but it can be formed. Drink some water, preferably warm water, take a walk, have a bowel movement. It is very essential for a healthy life that you empty the previous day's accumulation of poison and toxins from your body.

Then come some washes. In the nasal wash, you pour water through one nostril and it comes out from the other. Nasal wash cleans the inside of the nasal passages. The upper wash, in which a certain amount of hot water is drunk and vomited out, takes out all the toxins from the stomach. These washes are so healthy that prevention of diseases caused by malfunctioning of internal organs is achieved very easily and simply. There are a number of other washes that may be done occasionally. But the nasal wash should be done every day, especially in the allergy season or cold season and so on. Take some warm water with a little salt in it, just enough to make the water taste salty to match the salt in your tears. Do the nasal wash and see what it does for you.

Take a nice morning shower. In America it is a very good custom — a shower every day. But in Europe this is not common. The bath is not a traditional Western institution. When the Crusaders reconquered Spain and took it away from the Moors, in the city of Cordoba they found the baths that the Moors had built. They were considered works of the devil, and so these hundreds of baths were the first things that were destroyed by the Crusaders. In America, the morning shower is a very good thing to get your body clean. The custom in India is to take a shower or bath in the morning to start the day. Begin the day with a freshness, a clean force, and it will go a long way to make your day.

Then comes the physical exercise, *hatha yoga*. Some people prefer to do these before the shower; some, afterwards.

d) Breathing exercises, relaxation and meditation

Do your *pranayama*. Do the *nadi shodanan pranayama*, that is the channel purification, or the alternate nostril breathing. Do your relaxation. After relaxation, start meditation. It depends entirely on how much time you have. Go and sit on your meditation seat, be it for five minutes to refresh yourself. The relaxation will help you to wake up early in the morning. So take out five minutes extra for this experience without missing that five minutes of sleep.

e) Do not miss breakfast

Food is today's greatest tragedy. All kinds of diseases are brewing because of the wrong diet, refined processing and chemicals. A stranger walks into the supermarket and sees the lovely red apples. You tell him they are all sprayed with colour to look like that. Especially fine flour is a source of illness. Have roughage in your diet. Don't eat white bread; don't eat refined sugar. You'll find how much healthier you will feel.

DURING THE DAY

During the day, take a breather at lunch-time. Whenever you have time, count your breaths; be mindful; keep a watch over your emotions. If you are a doctor seeing patients, you owe yourself two minutes between patients to count your breaths. If you are a housewife going shopping, before receiving guests, you owe yourself two or three minutes to do nothing else but count your breaths and see what a change it makes for you. You forget your scarf in the supermarket and you go back for it; that takes more than two minutes. So don't say you don't have time. You have twenty-four hours and if you get five minutes late, it is permissible. You are in your right senses, when the guests arrive; your smile is not artificial and therefore you are really relaxed. Isn't that happier for them? So you owe yourself those few minutes of counting your breath whenever you can remember. Or if you have a *mantra*, repeat your *mantra* according to the methods taught.

IN THE EVENING

a) Wash

When you come home in the evening, you do not need to take a shower, but do the five-fold bath. Wash your feet, wash your hands, wash your face, and touch a wet cool hand to the back of your neck. You will feel refreshed. First the feet, because as you wash your feet, the heat rises up into your system. Wash your feet, wash your face, wash your hands and then relax, if you can give yourself the time.

b) Do the evening meditation

Always do your meditation before meals; not after meals so that you can breathe deeply without hearing the inner sounds.

c) Have an evening meal

After a meal, do whatever you have to do for the evening, for it is all yours.

WHEN POSSIBLE, ADD MASSAGE TO YOUR DAY

Since we lead a very busy life, it is not possible for us to do deep relaxation, complete physical yoga or a massage every day, but if we can do the complete set, perhaps twice a week, it would be very, very beneficial. Begin the day with a massage, as a massage is a very special art.

THERE ARE TWO ASPECTS OF MASSAGE

Massage with oil: Do not use chemical oils; use organic oils, such as mustard oil, coconut oil, etc. Just by exploring your body, you can learn to massage: feel your muscles, feel which muscles are long, round, where the effectiveness of massage can be felt in the fingertips, where it can be felt by using the palm, where it can be felt by using the edge or side of the hand and observe from head to toe. Learn to massage the spine by applying pressure between the vertebra by using both hands along the side of the spine.

After the massage, do the physical *asanas* or the physical postures. Your whole body will open up. Then lie down and do a long relaxation. You can listen to my taperecorded message after the postures. Then wash your body and sit in meditation. Especially when you are on a vacation, it is the best way to spend half a day with yourself, or with people you like doing it.

The other kind of massage is not done with oil and is called pressing. It is not rubbing, but pressing and is an entirely different procedure.

IN INDIA THERE ARE TWO RITUAL MASSAGES
By that I mean a regular habit. A child right from birth is massaged daily or is given an oil massage. A child is massaged from head to toe, before being put in a warm bath. There is a book *Birth Without Violence*, by Dr. LeBoyer, which describes the Indian system of child-birth. And his book, *Loving Touch* describes the Indian system of massaging babies. Massaging children daily will help accomplish wonderful neural-muscular development. As an adult, have someone massage you once or twice a week.

Another time we use massage is when we want to give love to our elders. And that kind is often done at night. We go to our parents, our mothers-in-law, fathers-in-law, to our *gurus*, our teachers, sit down near their feet, touch their feet and press their feet. The tiredness of the day and tension leaves them and then they talk of all their experiences and all their wisdom and so forth. When I want something from my *guru*, I go to him and I start pressing his feet. He says, "Yes, what do you want?" You have to know exactly how to press, which muscles. Even if you do not know the art, it is a good expression of love and respect and breaks a lot of barriers. Do that within the context of that respect and love and you will gain great blessings and grace from those who are wiser than you. Always seek that and you will lead a happy life.

PART FOUR

PSYCHOLOGICAL ASPECTS
OF MEDITATION

THE GIFT OF MEDITATION

At the still point of the turning world; neither flesh nor fleshless;
neither from nor towards; at the still point, there the dance is,
but neither arrest nor movement. And do not call it fixity,
where past and future are gathered.
Neither movement from nor towards,
neither ascent nor decline.
Except for the point, the still point, there would be no dance,
and there is only the dance.

— T.S. Eliot in **Four Quartets**

Every human being seeks relief from the unceasing motion of
daily life. We plan vacations, but we wind up taking all the chaos
of our lives with us. This is true even if we go to the wilderness,
because a noisy mind creates noise when it goes to a quiet place.

There is a quiet place you can go, without paying a penny, or
taking a plane, or driving to a cabin in the woods. That place
is within you. Yoga science says that the space between the outer
surface of the skin and the core — the centre of consciousness —
is far more vast, far more expansive, than the spaces between

the galaxies. Somewhere in that inner space, absolute quiet reigns supreme.

A human being is like a hurricane. On the outside, it's all agitation and excitation: whirlwind, lightning and thunderous rain. But there is a calm eye at the core.

At the 'still point of the turning world', from where the energy of the storm arises, the laws of the external world do not apply. It costs you nothing material to get there. The journey is instantaneous because you carry your shelter with you. It has no weight, and you can expand it to any size. What more could you want? When you let this inner calm pervade your being, you can envelop others in its sphere so that in your presence, even the angriest person becomes calm.

Learn to go beyond the surface turbulence of your personality, like an aerial dare-devil flying her plane into the eye of the storm. It requires no less courage, no less determination, no less resolution, to brave the storm of your personality and find the freedom within.

Freedom is peace, and peace is freedom. They are within your grasp anywhere, anytime you wish. This is the message of yoga. A person who has learned to go into the core of his being infuses all his faculties with power. Then, when he looks, he really sees.

FILLING WHAT ISN'T EMPTY

We are trained from childhood to think that our experiences go in from outside. We treat children like empty drums and begin pouring in 'education.' 'culture,' and 'training'. Pour in anything we see, pour in anything we read, anything we hear. Is this an exciting movie? Pour it in. Is it really frightening? By all means, pour it in — without discrimination, from the very first day.

Learn to go beyond the surface turbulence of your personality.

The philosophy of meditation does not ascribe to this doctrine of 'filling the drum', because the human being is already full. Without that fullness, it would be impossible to absorb sensations from outside. There is something within us that receives. Meditation is the way to discover what that something is. Sensations knock at the door, but someone inside has to say, 'Come in.' Who is that one? That being is who you really are. And that being, that consciousness, is eternal.

FINDING THE WAY IN

Some people think that meditation is a religious practice. But there is a fundamental difference between religion and meditation. In religion, we believe first and practice afterward. With meditation, we practice first and then believe. With religion, we swear by the book before we enter the church, temple, or mosque. But if we are a scientist, we don't stand outside the door of our physics lab with our head bowed, reciting, 'I solemnly believe in electrons, protons, and neutrons.' We walk into the lab and conduct an experiment and write out our inferences.

If the experiment succeeds, we write a book. It becomes a textbook, and everyone reads it. And yet, nobody holds it to the heart, saying, 'I swear by this book.'

Yoga and meditation are sciences. Meditators are taught to be dependent on no one and nothing — to be equally free of what gives us pleasure and pain.

The ancient texts say that if we are one, we are free. But if we have a servant, we are dependent. If we have ten servants, we are ten times more dependent. If we are a king with an army of 10,000, we are 10,000 times more dependent. And an emperor with an army of millions is that much more dependent. Now, what kind of sovereign is he who is a million times more dependent than the person who has nothing?

Understand the source of your dependence and the source of your pain. Don't be dependent on someone else's statement of truth, someone else's view of reality: 'I solemnly believe in God, because somebody told me God exists and it's here in the book. I believe there is a soul.' Where? Have you experienced it? Then what right have you to believe it?

The philosophy of meditation says, 'Find out' — not by logic, analysis, or rationalisation; not by collecting data and feeding them into a computer. Find out by experimenting. The secret of meditation is experimentation. The science of meditation has been practiced for thousands of years and taught in all great civilisations without a lot of fanfare. It was taught in Greece and in the China of antiquity, as well as in the lands that are now India and Japan. It was taught by teachers in the distant past exactly as it is taught today.

For thousands of years, the *yogis* of the Himalayan tradition have conducted experiments on guinea pigs. I, too, have a guinea pig and I've been experimenting on it for the last half a century — myself. What if I place my mind in this state of consciousness? What happens if I concentrate my mind on that? What happens if I arouse and maintain this particular emotion? What happens if I choose to eliminate this particular emotion and cultivate that other emotion for the next six months? What happens if I concentrate on a flame? What happens if I remain aware of my breathing?

In the laboratory of the mind, there are a million

possible experiments. Whatever you think, you will become; it requires no complicated equipment. But it does require somebody who can give you direction, someone who can tell you, 'On Highway One, north, you will reach such and such a place.' But if you stand on that highway, hold the directions in your hand, and chant, 'I solemnly believe in the validity of these directions,' will you get anywhere? No, you have to get in the car and drive. You have to work on yourself. And you have to work independently of external conditioning, free of all that has been fed to you. There must be some time in your daily schedule when you are truly free of your surroundings, both externally and mentally. Only then can you experience what is yours, what was always yours, and what will always be yours — unpolluted, immutable, unaffected, unchanged, and unaltered.

ACHIEVING HARMONY

Yoga and meditation science lead you to unaltered states of consciousness. Altered states are not the goal, as they involve one emotion this minute, another the next; deep sleep, shallow sleep, horrible dreams, lovely dreams, desires, sensations, pleasures, and pains. Constant alteration, constant change. The unaltered state is the eternal state, not subject to past, present, or future.

Meditation is the art of training the mind to produce harmony. The same situation that produces stress in one person will have no effect on the trained meditator who has strengthened his nervous system and purified his mind. Such a person can achieve mundane goals more easily too, because a 'neat' mind with little or no confusion can make better decisions more quickly. When you feel tense, you can't make a decision; or you make the wrong decisions, in matters big and small.

When you learn the art of relaxation and meditation, you will experience clarity of mind, because you are not receiving conflicting messages. The more difficult the situation facing a meditator, the calmer he becomes. A meditator knows calmness is the best way to deal with a tough problem and has the mastery to act from this knowledge.

Keep moving within, until you encounter the still point, the eye of the storm.

A clear mind knows what to say. The right words come out in the right tone and the right manner. Your body language changes, and the people around you respond to you differently, without knowing why. Your family dynamics change, your job situation changes. You draw a positive response from others, because you've learned to draw the right response from within yourself.

Yogic meditation begins with correct breathing, because breath is the link between body and mind. The states of breath are symptoms of the states of mind and health. Observe the waves of your breath, and learn to direct them. Learn to make your breath flow in harmony, so the jerkiness of the mind and emotions ceases. A few moments of calm breathing will help you overcome intense emotions. Train yourself daily to calm your breathing.

That is the preliminary, the first step, in the journey. Keep moving within, until you encounter the still point, the eye of the storm. When you do, you'll have a direct experience of the benefits of meditation. You'll be grateful for having found the quiet you have been craving for all your life. And that is only the beginning.

CHAPTER 2

MEDITATION FOR OTHER'S SAKE

I want to bring you back, away from what the urban industrial civilisation and its corporate structures and workplace require- ments have done to your psychology and your reactions. Sometimes I get very sad about it, because the rest of the world keeps reinforcing this 'me' in you. And once a year you hear something like this, and at that time you say, 'Yes, we'd like to elevate ourselves' and so on. But you go back into that world and it's again the same thought pattern. It keeps getting reinforced. And people do not step out of this 'me' syndrome. Without stepping out of this 'me' syndrome, there is no meditation. Meditation is dropping the 'me.' What do I get out of it? What do I receive from it? What benefits come to me? And now today I heard a new phrase I hadn't heard before — 'yoga entrepreneurship' or 'yoga fashion', or something comprising of pictures of someone in yoga poses, in a very glamorous form. Underneath, the credit line ran 'Suit designed by...', 'photograph taken by...' No, it's no joke. And yoga magazines and all... people add glamour. This is very painful to me.

I'm not against the signboard of the wineshop. There was

this wandering sage who came to a village. And when people hear of someone holy, sacred, they just come to pay respects. And they don't come to say, 'What's in it for me? What benefit will I get by seeing him?' They just come for his *darshan*. My whole childhood was spent that way. I'd travel from city to city and people would just come. There was no question; they're not there to ask for help for something, nor to ask for solutions to their problems. They're there just to be there, just to sit in the orbit, called *darshan*. And nobody comes empty handed. And that's how I spent my childhood; that was my cultural conditioning. And I'll tell you a very personal secret. I struggled with the question of whether to tell you or not. Half the cause of my illness is people's cultural self-centredness and confrontational attitude, and harsh tone of the voice, and me, me, me — 'Solve my problems', 'do a therapy with me'. And I have to soothe everyone and take their conflicts and sorrows inside me. And I like to spread joy; I don't like to share my sadness, but there is this sadness in me — for you, about you, about your self-created pains, about your self-created suffering. Meditation is NOT a therapy. It's not for *gaining* something. It's not a secret of success. Don't do self-centred meditation. Transcend this molecular shield, into which the live consciousness-essence, the conscious life-essence that is you, has infused itself to make this molecular shield bcome alive and have a semblance of awareness. Whether I succeed or I fail, I am going to keep trying to say this. Enough therapy, and enough benefits! 'Entrepreneurial yoga', or 'yoga entrepreneurial' — my mouth gets stuck! The word doesn't want to come out of my mouth. A curse word! We are *not* into *success*, *successful* centres, *successful* classes! Transcendence. Success will come incidentally if you abandon the claims to benefits. Then the benefits will flow, and you will take those benefits and share them. You will take from the basket and throw to the world. Step out of this block if you want to make progress.

You know, I have no time to meditate for myself. I really don't. Because I promise so many people: "I will pray for you." And on my list there are always 300 to 400 people every day. I have to find time for that. The prayer in meditation is a whole different art. It's even subtler than the use of the *mantra*. And the *yogis* pray not the way the religious people pray. The way the religious people pray is not the way the *yogis* pray. Eliminate your conflicts and angers while inhaling a sense of wisdom, love and grace. That is the preparation for the next step. And that is exhaling beauty, love, energy, compassion, and sending it to the entire universe. It is inhalation of the pain and the suffering and the conflict of the entire universe, and being able to absorb it inside – dissipating it inside. That's just the beginning of the meditational prayer. Meditational prayer, for anyone, takes less than a quarter second to achieve the full result. It's non-verbal; it's a form of including someone in your field. The way we sit here and meditate together, what happens? Every mind, all the minds join the *guru*-field. All the minds, join the *guru*-field and a single field is created.

There are two kinds of group meditations. One group meditation is when people gather at the same *time*, at the same *place*, and sit together. That is one kind. The other is, people gather together at the same *time*. That's all. And that way you can have a global group meditation, if you wish. You have a problem in the centre? The place where meditation is held will become a meditation centre. If it is held under a tree, that place will become the meditation centre. A meditation centre is *not* a place. A meditation centre is a *time*, when everyone meditates together. And let it *not* be self-centred meditation.

We need to re-define all these texts, all these books, all these charts, the nature and functions of the mind, the five manifest functions of the mind, the seven unmanifest functions of the mind, the *antakarana*, the sixteen *kalas*, the seventeen components of the subtle body and the five *koshas*. But, when the Lord God and the *guru* come to claim your soul, they're not going to ask you, 'Which are the sixteen *kalas* according to the *Aitareya Upanishad*, chapter two, verse three or two, or whatever?' Even if you know it all by heart, don't identify too closely with it. Learn it. You need to know it, because you need to have a clear perception. Don't identify with your intellectual information — 'I'm a great scholar.' No, my master *beat* it out of me — "All the scholarly things and philosophical discussions you do," he said, "whom does it benefit?" So, at a certain place, even though we *have* the information, our humility, our egolessness, tells us not to exhibit it unless it is helpful to someone. The meditation that is not self-centred is a secret. It is a linkage with the *guru*-field; it is a linkage with the universal energy-field, not for the purpose of drawing energy into 'me'; not for the purpose of receiving the healing power from the universe. That is all ego-enhancement. Surrender to the universal energy-field. Unblock. The power will come gushing and eventually you'll be able to use it for the benefit of others.

And when you want to learn to pray for others, just a little wave from your mind will go to that mind. It takes one-quarter of a second. And that is all healing. If you can visit them personally, fine, because at this stage it is difficult for you to actually transmit that way. Sometimes at the meditation centre, when I know that a resident is disturbed, I quietly creep into his bedroom while he is asleep, and I sit down by his side and meditate. I don't have time to do meditation for *my* progress: 'Am I progressing, Master?' Maybe you can tell me, but I don't know whether I'm progressing or not; improving my meditation or deepening my meditation. Maintain pure spirituality, that's all.

If you have that, the therapy will happen. Whether you do a scientific study on the effect of meditation on blood pressure or not, blood pressure will be improved anyway. We're planning science conferences and everything. It's all out there. It's like the sage who wandered into a village and sat down. Everybody came for the *darshan*, for sitting in the holy company, and all were happy to see the sage. Then came a person looking very sad. On being asked the reason for his sadness, he said, "Master, I'm not sad for myself; I'm sad for my brother. He's the only one in the village who hasn't come to see you. He's a notorious drunkard, and unless there is drinking, he won't go anywhere. I know that if he only came to you, he would change, but he won't come." The sage replied, "Oh, I see. Alright. Never mind." So the sage wandered off, and a few months later he came by again. He occupied a little cottage, and hung outside the cottage a board saying 'The New Village Wineshop'. And the brother of the sad person, passing by, said, "Oh, the new village wineshop?" He walked in and their eyes met. *That* inebriation cannot be equalled to 10,000 bottles of the best Napa, Californian wine.

We have a saying, among the Sufi poets: 'Why do you drink the wine from which inebriation wears off? Drink wine that you drink once and you never get un-inebriated.'

Is it *possible* to do something without seeking, without inquiring about its benefits? Is it *possible* to do something without looking for its uses, just for the sake of transcendence? You can do it!

Meditate as an experience of the *heart* — the way you feel love inside your *heart*. And let that be a *feeling*, 'Am I doing it right? Is this the technique? Is this what he said? Is this the sequence?' What's the *right technique* for a child to cry for mother's milk? What's the *right technique* for a child, this baby infant, to express his thanks for the mother's milk? Exactly how wide should he stretch his mouth to smile at the mother?

The techniques emerge through natural experience. Description of the experience is the technique. But the experience cannot be gained by technique alone. Please remember the method, the technique comes *out* of the description of the experience. And that is how all of *hatha yoga* has originated. It is a description of the events that have happened in the *prana* body, which has then moved the physical body, and brought changes in the physical body. But by technique, you will not learn to awaken the *prana*. You will still have to go into the *experience*. Simply by placing the body in that position, you will not gain the benefit. You can use all the ropes and all the pulleys to put the body in this shape or that. Yoga is self-dependence. If yoga requires ropes and pulleys and props, it's no yoga. The only rope it requires is the breath. The *nadis* are ropes enough.

Use all the tools of the modern world, but don't identify with them. They are only tools. They are not your identity. They are *not* the identity of yoga. They are *not* the identity of meditation.

Use the *tools* of the 21st century to spread the *message* of the 21st century BC. Do not try to *corrupt and dilute* the 21st century BC by identification with the *tools* of the 21st century AD. It is the careful trapeze artist's tightrope walking that you *have* to learn to do.

Initially, my moral crisis arose when teaching at an institution for a fixed amount of money and selling the *Upanishads*, *Vedas*, *sutras* and *mantras*. It was a very unhappy time for me. I could never come to terms with it. Because in my tradition we would go to the *guru's ashram* at the age of five and study under him. The fruits of the *ashram* trees feed us. You go out once a day, and back in the village, receive your alms, come back. You serve, you graze his cows, you tend to his trees, sit and receive knowledge. There are no taperecorders. And our master taught us in private.

A few months before he left his body, my communication with him changed greatly, and he had trained me to ask my questions in as few words as possible. So I would labour on my question, 'Which syllable I can cut out? How much can I reduce it further?' Because if you know the core of your question, you know half the answer. People don't know how to ask a question. And when people send me a six-page letter, I don't reply. And they get very hurt. So I would sit, collect my questions, and ask for an audience. And I would say, 'Swamiji, can I see you?'

'Yes, come, come, come, Son, come.' So I would give him the question.

He would say, 'Okay, second question.'

So I would give him the second question. And he would answer: 'Third question'.

Four, five, six questions. Each time the same answer. 'Any more questions?'

'No, *Swamiji*.'

'Alright. Go.'

But then he also taught me how to listen to the answer. And that is what is guiding me.

For the last twenty-five years we've been seeing him. Any time of the day or night if one walked into his room, the TV would be on. All twenty-four hours he had the TV on! And we'd just wonder. Someone asked him about it. He said, "Well, when people come to me, they forget to look at me; they start looking at the TV, and then I work on their minds." When you approach the *guru*, what he's doing is not your concern. Your concern is to have your mind on the *guru*.

The meaning of the word 'Upanishad' is 'to sit very close and near'. Sit in your master or *guru's* energy field; sit inside his heart. That is *Upanishad*.

If you are a teacher, representing the lineage, you are responsible for the progress of your students, to lead them to the next step, beyond what you are able to offer. You know how far you can take your student. Then you should know where to take him further.

We have a legend in India which says that if you have knowledge and you don't pass it on, you become a *Brahma-rakshas*. or a Brahman-demon. I don't want to be *Brahma-rakshas*, so I have to pass on the knowledge before I die. The tradition is, if you want to give others knowledge, *you* clothe *them*, *you* feed *them*, *you* raise *them*. *You* establish *them*. *You* worry about *them*. But you have to be a disciple; not a selfish student looking for therapy, for benefits, for uses, or as some, who are here only to get information from me, to go back and only use that information.

When you take a benefit, you naturally give something, and that is a divine gift.

If you want the lineage to help you, to guide your spiritual progress, stay very carefully on a very well-charted path of personal purity. And do *not* use yoga for exterior purposes. And if you *do* practice and *do* teach purely as a spiritual calling, then your exterior purposes, I promise, will be taken care of.

Simply feel the flow and the touch of your breath in your nostrils. Exhale and inhale gently, slowly, smoothly. When you come to the end of a breath, let there be no pause. With the *mantra* wave flowing, resolve in your mind that for the next two minutes, there will be no interrupting thoughts, and there will be no pause between the breaths. Make the resolve and begin now. Without breaking the flow, gently open your eyes. Maintain the flow.

CHAPTER 3

PRAYING THROUGH MEDITATION

In externalised and ritualised religions, the prayer is outward and aloud. The louder we shout perhaps, God hears us better! Has God turned deaf that we have to shout our prayers aloud? The source from which the religions and all the traditions of spiritual philosophies arise is in the calmest state of the mind, the undisturbed states of consciousness. Not that consciousness can ever be disturbed; only the mind is disturbed. *Chit shakti* is never disturbed, but because the mind is disturbed we assume that *chit shakti* is disturbed. All the traditions of prayers, religions and spiritual philosophies have arisen from that deepest state of mind that the founders of the traditions have entered. The following stories amply prove this theory:

Jesus spent forty days in the wilderness. Moses climbed the mountain and his face glowed so radiantly that the onlookers could not look at it directly and he had to cover his face. Zarathushtra attained enlightenment after ten years in the cave. Buddha sat absolutely still for forty-nine days and forty-nine nights under the *bodhi tree*. The message of the Himalayan *yogis* is that you too can enter that state and for entering that state, you do not need to withdraw into a Himalayan cave. There is only one cave for you to meditate in. This portable cave is called your body. Learn to enter that cave and you will need no more pilgrimages.

I have spoken on the divergences and convergences in the meditative traditions. According to the knowledge that I have imbibed from my master, Swami Rama of the Himalayas, there are as many entrances into this cave as there are aspects, powers, faculties, that constitute our personality and in each one of these lies a valid path. You can enter through the eyes; you can enter through the pours of your body.

All the traditions are part of a vast system within which there are sub-systems; there are methods and pathways, uncountable but interconnected sequentially. A master is one who has mastered not one system, or one sub-system, but who has mastered all the vast systems. One practice that seems to run in almost all meditative traditions of the world is that of right breathing.

The entire Buddhist tradition of meditation starts with the practice of breath awareness. *Kumbaka*, retention of the breath, goes up to 60,000 seconds at a time in certain very advanced exercises but you can hold only what you have. At present you have no breath. You have gasps, not breath. Every breath is jerky. Where is the breath? Where is the flow? One of the fundamental definitions of meditation, both in the Vedantic texts and the yoga texts, is *pratiaya katanata* which in the Vedanta becomes *samana prataya pravaha*. Shankaracharya, in his commentary on the *Bhagavad Gita* says "*Samana prataya pravaha itraa pratiya anantri taha.*" The even flow is obtained by the practice of observation of the flow of the breath but then the breath has to flow and cannot be a series of jerks.

In diaphramatic breathing, we first train people so that the breath flows from the seat of *prana*, from the navel centre and returns to the same. The other part is the even flow and there are definitions of what 'even flow' actually means. We go into the subtleties of these in the training of our students and disciples. *Samana pravaha* is uninterrupted flow. In the Buddhist meditative tradition, there are numerous paths. The Zen masters teach it slightly differently from the Tibetan masters. Tibetan masters teach it quite differently from the Theravada Southern School masters of Burma and Thailand and so on. It is part of the *anusatti* system, which I teach at my *ashram* also, from the text *Visuddhi Maga* of *Budha Gosha*, which is the primary text of the Buddhist meditative tradition. There are more advanced texts in the Tibetan tradition translated from the original Sanskrit, like the text of *Natapada*, *Naropa* and so on.

For observing the breath, always begin with calming yourself and bringing your attention to the vessel of your body. Observing the temple of God, calm the mind so that it permeates your whole body. Normally it is best to go through a relaxation practice. If you do not do so, all the thoughts and emotions that you store in your neuro-muscular system will be released and you will perceive them as external or interrupting thoughts in meditation. If you do not fully relax, all the thoughts and emotions that you store in your neuro-muscular system will be released during meditation and they will become your interrupting thoughts.

Simply relax your forehead, jaw, shoulders, throat centre, heart centre, navel centre, thigh joints, and all the way down to your toes; in ascending order — your leg muscles, your thigh joints, the entire area surrounding the navel, heart area, throat area, speech area, the jaw and forehead. Always relax.

Now feel the flow of breath and observe the gentle rise and fall of your stomach and the navel area as you exhale how that area gently relaxes. As you inhale, it slightly contracts. Breathe gently, slowly and smoothly. Continue to let your breath flow smooth without a jerk, without a break between the breaths.

Another variation of it is exhaling and inhaling while feeling the movement of the stomach and the navel region. Think of the *mantra* of the divine name you choose. Let your primary focus remain in observing the gentle movement of the stomach and the navel area so that your *sankalpa* may draw the *prana* from the navel *chakra* and awaken that region.

Now a third variation. Feel the flow from the navel to the nostrils in a slim and narrow channel of consciousness. Exhale and inhale smoothly on a path that is *basitum tunibham*, as fine as a slim fibre from the lotus root. First experiment without a *mantra*, only feeling the pathway of the breath and then experiment with the variation. While chanting the *mantra*, feel the pathway of the breath from the navel to the nostrils. Allow no break between the breaths.

In the next variation, only feel the flow of your breath in your nostrils without a *mantra*; exhale and inhale, breathing gently, slowly, smoothly. For those who are already initiated in the Himalayan tradition, it is most difficult to do without a *mantra*, but try you must.

Next variation, especially for those who do not wish to believe in a divine name or *mantra* involves the following. While exhaling, count in your mind one and while inhaling, count two. Continue to feel the breath in the nostrils and keep counting one and two. In the next variation, exhale by counting one, inhale at two, exhale at three, inhale at four and exhale at five. Again inhale at five, exhale at four, inhale at three, exhale at two, inhale at one, and thus maintain the flow and the count.

Now replace the count with a divine name or a sacred phrase from whichever religion it is. Breathing gently with no break between the breaths, feel the flow in the nostrils, maintaining the same thought flow. Maintain the flow and observe how the breath and the mind flow together as a single stream.

Without breaking the awareness of the flow, gently open your eyes. Maintain the variations even with your eyes open.

Let me now take you through the first practices in *swara yoga* or the yoga of breath rhythms. Relax all your senses. Establish diaphragmatic breathing. You cannot do these practices with your chest closed or with crossed arms. Sit as you should sit with your arms separate, hands separate and relax. Establish diaphragmatic breathing from the navel and bring your awareness to your nostrils and again to your nostrils to feel which of your nostrils flows more forcefully. Only one of them flows forcefully. It changes its rhythm every one hour forty-five minutes or so and if you cannot distinguish, then start with the left nostril. Just feel the flow of the breath in your left nostril with the count of one and two or with count of one to five, five to one or with your *mantra* or divine name. Whichever variety you prefer at this time, just feel the flow in your left nostril. Do not allow any break in the thought you choose. Now feel the breath flow in your right nostril with the same one thought of the count or the name. Now merge the flow in both the nostrils. Continue to feel the flow and gently open your eyes without breaking the flow.

This is again the beginning of another system within which there are numerous sub-systems, including the exercise for memory improvement.

Sit back, place your hands lightly on your knees, elbows close to you; your shoulders should be relaxed so that your chest may expand. Close your eyes and go home to the seat of your consciousness. Relax. Take the word *so-ham*, inhale with *so*; exhale with *ham*. With your neuro-muscular system completely relaxed, establish an even flow of the breath.

Now feel as though your breath is flowing through your entire body, from the crown of your head down to your toes and from the toes to the crown. Feel as though your whole body is breathing from top to toes and toes to top evenly, gently and smoothly. What you now feel is the *prana rupti*.

This practice is a basic essential for *brahmacharya*. Inhaling from the thigh joints, from the perineum, ascend and exhale from the crown with *so-ham*. Inhale as though you are inhaling from the navel centre with the thought *so-ham* and exhale from the crown, activating your navel *chakra* and letting the energy ascend very gently as though there is a red flame in the navel centre from where you're ascending with the breath. Exhaling from the crown, inhale as though from the cavity in the heart centre in the lower chest between the breasts where there is a cave filled with a *jyotirlinga*. Exhale and inhale, ascending with the breath from the *anahata chakra* and with *so-ham*; exhale as though from the crown.

Inhale as though you're inhaling from the centre between the eyebrows, where there is a crystal-like pure flame; with *so-ham* inhale and exhale as though from the crown. Imagine you're inhaling from the centre between the eyebrows. Exhale from the crown into infinity with *so-ham*. Now return as though you're inhaling and exhaling through your whole body. *The so-ham* sound should permeate with the distribution of *prana* through the entire body, from the crown to the toes and toes to the crown.

There are some human beings who re-attune themselves to the subtler subconscious system. That is what meditation is all about. One of the great spiritual lady preachers of India — Amrithanandamaya Ma has a huge *ashram* and almost a city of 10,000 people. She is widely known as *Ammaji*, the respected Mother. Two or three hours before the tsunami came, she ordered the entire place to be vacated. She sent her *ashram* members to run all over the beach to chase the fishermen away and no one died in that area.

DOES GOD HAVE ANY LOGIC?

If we could understand that logic, our own lives, our own emotions would not be so chaotic.

But if we keep our meditation only as a medicine for headache, we will never understand God's logic.

That knowledge is accessible to you, but it needs many changes in the way you have looked at the world — the micro world, or your body.

There are two paths in yoga: The path from outside in and the path from inside out.

In the *Philosophy of Hatha Yoga*, I have explained the *hatha yoga* path from inside out.

Let me explain to you what breath is, but before that you need to know what you are.

You are *atman* — a wave of the divine light-force; a wave, not an isolated particle.

This wave does not need a lamp or a star to illuminate it. Its light does not arise by converting hydrogen into helium.

- It is self-luminous
- It is light that is consciousness
- It has no name, no condition; no gender, no time

When a *yogi* warns his *ashram* two hours or four hours before a disaster, he is not looking into the future because in that *atman* there is no time.

So he or she is seeing this in the no-time zone. Learn to enter the no-time zone. It has nothing to do with the power of prediction because prediction implies future time.

But we are not talking about the time today; only about breath.

Some day I will tell you what time is in the study of yoga.

It is not what I see in the watch.

It is not from morning to night.

You, the *atman*, live in a house, when the divine transcendent being sends forth a wave that is you.

If you wanted a very pure home for this wave — a beautiful home — nothing can match the luminosity of this wave.

If you enter a cave, which has never been entered before — where no jerky air has ever entered, in that deep cave you come across a pool of water. That pool of water has been there for 10,000 years, and no heavy breeze has ever touched it. It does not know what a wave is and it cannot imagine what a liquid might be.

That is the interior of that most beautiful, secret place that I was talking about.

From outside the cave you cannot imagine the depth of that place in silence.

DO YOU WANT TO KNOW WHERE THAT PLACE IS?

It is in the deep interior of your mind. Go to that.

That is the material of which the house is built and in which the *atman* wave of the divine dwells.

The interior of that wall is clearer than any crystal — such a crystal into which no shadow of any object ever falls. The outside wall of that beautiful house is not so pure. But that wall is further protected by another wall. That other wall is called the *prana*.

Prana is the house inside which the mind's house is built — inside which you, the self-luminous *atman*, live. But these forces of mind and *prana* are yet too subtle to operate in the earthly world. They need an earthly medium in order to manipulate the earthly surroundings around it.

Now imagine a brilliant light. It is covered with a white cloth, white curtain or white lamp-shade. That white lamp-shade is covered by another yellow lamp-shade. And that by a pink one, and that by a red one, that by a green one, and that by a blue one and all of those lamp-shades are covered with a thick black lamp-shade.

And you are outside that lamp-shade. What colour light do you see?

This is how invisible your own light is to your outer, earthly surface.

You need to go through a dance of seven veils to drop one veil after another to know who you are.

This *atman*, the divine self that is a wave of the transcendent in its nature, is entirely different and beyond what mind, *prana* and body can do. The *atman* has no limitation of time, space or light.

Every wave that is you, is linked to the infinite transcendant whose wave you are. A ray of your light or the *atman* is sent forth.

Those who need language have given that ray the name *kundalini*.

This wave may be compared with the laser beam, which might be used to trigger some mechanism. This wave, that is the mind, says, "My dear mind, let me make you even more beautiful." And it sends forth awareness and knowledge into the mind. That light filters through the many veils of the mind. To the mind this wave is the sentience of consciousness.

The mind has no consciousness. In *samkhya*, which is the basic philosophic system of yoga, mind is not a spiritual force. The mind is the finest product of *prakriti*, Nature — finer than all the forces the physicists can measure in laboratories. So never confuse mind with *atman*.

The first step in self-realisation is to understand that point. When you think of the conditions of mind as though they are the conditions of *atman*, you live in very, painful ignorance.

The mind receives its semblance of awareness by the touch of that laser beam, the *kundalini*, that flows forth from you, the *atman*. Through all the layers of the mind, that ray is filtered and comes out at the other end in a very, very diluted form.

The ray continues and touches *prana*. It gives to *prana* the semblance of being alive.

Consciousness and life are your nature. Only the slimmest rays of that light and consciousness are passed on to the mind and *prana*.

You can increase the strength of these beings if you so wish. The process of doing this is called meditation.

This *prana* is housed in a very tangible, visible, physical body. When the mind and *prana* vibrate rhythmically, the vibration of waves that is you, the *atman*, is passed through your body, which at present, you say, 'This is me'.

This is not 'you'. You are only operating this mechanism by the three-fold *shakti* — *iccha shakti*, *janna shakti* and *kriya shakti*.

When the mind and *prana*, charged by the vibration of the *atman* wave, touch the softer tissues of your body, the softer tissues begin to move in response to the rhythm of *prana*, mind, *kundalini* and *atman*. As they begin to pulsate — that which would have been some pocket of dead air trapped in these hollows — that air begins to flow. This is called breath. This is the journey of consciousness up to your tangible breath. The relationship of breath to all the other tissue organs is explained by medical science. But the connection of this breath with the consciousness and the light force, going all the way to *atman*, is described by the meditation science.

An advanced meditator, who knows the self to be this *atman*, the wave, has total control of the volume and intensity of knowledge and life force that pass through, on those surfaces where the *atman* wave makes its manifestation in the form of breath.

That is the yoga path from inside out. At present you are struggling on a path from outside inward, from breath to *atman*.

There are two ways to explore a river: you can start from its source in the mountains and go all the way to the ocean. Or you can start at the ocean end and pass through the plains and the mountains to the source of the river.

The path of popular yoga is the path of going from the ocean to the mountain. The path of meditational yoga is the path of going from the Himalayas to the oceans of the world. That is what we call Himalayan *hatha yoga*. Take this perception into your silence. Learn to take the interior path. Your *asanas* will become a manifestation of that *atman*, the wave.

It is that wave that moves your body in such an even-flowing rhythm. If your *atman* is not an even-flowing dance of the wave of divine energy, it becomes an exercise, not yoga.

PART FIVE

ADVANCED MEDITATION

CHAPTER 1

SUBTLETIES IN MEDITATION PRACTICE AND PHILOSOPHY

SUBTLETIES IN BREATH AWARENESS

Many impatient aspirants seek advanced practices of breathing and meditation. They want to jump to the next higher ground without having mastered the present one prescribed by their meditation guide. The authentic traditions do not rush to the next higher ground but rather establish the base firmly, trying the disciple's patience and endurance for long. The core principle is *anu-shasana* (discipline), without which one does not become a *shishya* (disciple). The *Yoga-sutras* of Patanjali say:

"*Sa tu dirgha-kala-nairantarya-satkara-asevito drdha-bhumih.*"

This practice, however, becomes firm of ground only when pursued and maintained in assiduous and complete observance for a long time, without any interruption and with a positive and devout attitude.

Having undertaken observance for a decade or two, or a lifetime, does not necessarily constitute mastery. The tests of the mastery are as follows:

The technique, *kriya*, itself is perfected. For example, every time one practices breath awareness, one does not fail even for an instant in maintaining it by its full definition, such as:

- No noise in the breath
- No jerks
- Equal duration of exhalation and inhalation
- Equal force in exhalation and inhalation
- No tension arising during inhalation (which is the norm with most unproficient practitioners)
- Greater awareness of the exhalation process than that of inhalation
- Towards the end of each breath, preparing the mind to observe the transition to the next breath, thus eliminating/mastering the pause that would otherwise occur
- Absolutely no interruption nor break in the breath and its awareness throughout a given meditation session
- When one has moved up to the next higher practice of breath awareness, such as equal force of breath in both nostrils, or inhalation and exhalation in the ratio of 1:2 respectively, then, experience of the same uninterrupted perfection in the flow and observation throughout a session occurs

- Being able to enter the same practice without any preliminaries anytime, anywhere that one may wish, and under any kind of surroundings or company or situation, and maintaining the same perfection throughout
- Being able to maintain the process of the practice perfectly and without any interruption, irrespective of one's physical and mental condition, circumstances and surroundings, for as long as one wishes

- Entering every time, without fail, the highest or deepest state of serenity, silence and stillness that this particular *kriya* is capable of imparting, without having to make any special endeavour; the practice becomes easy and natural
- Being able to remain in that highest or deepest state, uninterrupted, without coming into the shallows, for as long as one wishes, irrespective of any other internal or external situation
- That state becomes one's normal baseline awareness, one's natural ground of consciousness. Formerly one had to enter into and regress from that state. Now there is no regression to lower states that were previously one's common ground and have now been left behind. One has now built one's meditation hut, as it were, on a higher *bhumi*, plateau
- It is at this point one may guide others' meditations up to that particular degree but not claim the powers beyond for the sake of ego display, glamour, publicity, higher class fees, etc. Such guided group meditations do not constitute an initiation into a higher state; they are conducted only to show the students in the group a glimpse of what they need to and can attain through their own practice – if they truly aspire. Discipleship is a long-term spiritual entrepreneurship
- One has now become qualified, gained the *adhikara*, to grant initiation up to that level. This means that one may transmit that state to a qualified student only and thereby change his level of consciousness
- Then and only then the next subtlety of the practice may be imparted. From here one will again begin the process of climbing up and coming down for the next higher ground,

next deeper level of serenity till all the above eight tests are progressively passed. That higher ground again becomes one's normal state. And so one keeps 'progressing' till the ultimate peak is reached

The mastery is achieved not by jumping to advanced techniques one after the other, but rather by going into the subtleties. Here are some of the most important subtleties in the practice of breath awareness:

One starts the practice session after one has

- loosened the major knots of tension in the body, breath and mind, through joints and glands exercises, basic *asanas* (yoga postures), as prescribed and as feasible
- Relaxation practices, such as the ones in *shavasana*
- Establishing the diaphragmatic breathing
  - in *makara-asana* (crocodile position)
  - in *shavasana* (corpse position)
  - in sitting position

The practice of diaphragmatic breathing is not to be reserved only for the meditation session. This should become one's normal breathing for all hours.

- The basic rules for sitting need to be followed — straight spine; head, neck and trunk aligned. A straight spine is not a straight line but a slight S-curve, as seen in a skeleton hanging in a doctor's office
  - The knees should not be above the waistline, and both knees should be equidistant from the ground
  - The shoulders should be even
  - The neck should not be bent forward, backward or sideways, nor the chin lifted up

- No strain on the eyes to place them in some artificial position
- Neither smile nor a scowl. In the Ajanta caves in west India, there is a statue of the Buddha in meditation. If one shines a light on it from a reflector on to its left side, the face appears sad. If the light is reflected on to the right side, it looks joyous. If the light is reflected on to the centre of the face, it is serene. This is what true meditation is
- No feeling of tension in the spine and the neck. If there is such a feeling, adjust the height of the cushion you are sitting on to elevate the pelvis and check the position of the spine

- Check the state of your relaxation. It is not always necessary to go through the entire relaxation procedure. If one has been practising relaxation procedures for some time, the relaxed state of the neuro-muscular system should become a normal habit. An abbreviated version of the progressive relaxation may suffice
  - Relax your forehead. It is not possible for thoughts of worries, anxieties, fears, aggression and so forth to arise in the mind if the forehead is kept relaxed. It is one sure way of freeing the mind from the possibility of such negative thoughts that interrupt the flow of meditation
  - Relax the hinges of the jaw. This eliminates the inclination to disturb the mental silence through speech. No sub-vocalisation or vocalisation will occur
  - Relax the throat centre. This re-inforces at a subtler level what is achieved through the relaxation of the hinges of the jaw at a more tangible level

- Relax the shoulders. This will relax the entire active organ of the hand, eliminating the inclination towards manual activity
- Relax the heart centre. This will replace the disturbed and negative emotions with a gentle and serene sentiment and the heart will thus no longer feed disturbing thoughts into the mind. Gradually the feeling of *dahara-akasha*, an internal field of space, develops
- Relax the navel region. This will preclude the inclinations for all sorts of ingestion, desires to assimilate into oneself what is externally introduced. It will also release the knots of *prana*-force so that the *prana* may flow unhindered, thus supporting the smooth flow of the breath-mind stream
- Relax the thigh joints. This will eliminate the inclination for locomotion
- Once again, relax all these points in reverse, coming back to the relaxed forehead
- Maintain the relaxed state throughout, so that if someone surprises you by lifting your arm, the arm drops like a dead log
- A body thus relaxed will enter a state of natural stillness. There will neither ensue a feeling of swaying, swirling and so forth, nor would the body uncontrollably twitch or move about
- Here the practice of breath awareness begins. Simply observe the gentle rise and fall of the navel and the stomach region with the gentle rhythm of breathing. Here one may remember one's *mantra* along with the breath, or a sacred prayer word or name of God from one's own tradition: merge

the same as a thought (not vocalised or sub-vocalised) with the breath flow. Keep to this phase as long as one wishes. Normally a word is chosen that may flow smoothly with the breath, such as *so-ham* (same as *hamso*)

- Then, observe the pathway of the breath from the navel to the nostrils, again, with the sacred word. It is a very subtle and narrow pathway of energy, like a thin streak of brilliant lightning or like the edge of a sword. In more advanced stages of subtlety, it is described as ten-thousandth of a hairbreadth. Keep to this phase as long as you wish
    - Feel the flow of breath in your passive nostril, for a certain number of breaths — three, seven, eleven or whatever
    - Feel the flow of breath in the active nostril for the same number of breaths
- Now, feel the flow and touch of the breath in both the nostrils, together with the sacred word-thought. Feel where the breath touches the mucous membranes. Keep to this phase as long as you wish
- Observe how the breath, word-thought and the mind flow together as a single stream. Keep this observation as long as you wish
- Observe how the whole mind, and the entire consciousness becomes a smooth-flowing stream
- Initially this phase would elude one but slowly one begins to glimpse the mind stream without resorting to the breath flow. There the true meditation begins

Many other possible steps are not included in the above scheme, like ninety-six basic varieties of *nadi-shodhana* channel purification or alternative nostril breathing.

SUBTLETIES

Without relaxing the body, and keeping it relaxed without establishing diaphragmatic breathing, without calming the emotional states of the heart, without constantly observing the state of the breath, the breath will not flow smoothly.

Commonly, everyone has the habit of becoming tense during inhalation. Watch out for the involuntary tensions developing during the inhalations, and consciously relax during each inhalation until such time that the inhalation-phase tension ceases to be a habit.

Permit no noise in the breath flow. Let the breath be even, by three definitions:

- No jerk is felt in breathing
- The duration of exhalation and inhalation is equal
- The force in the exhalation and the inhalation is equal

Exhalation and inhalation are made equal in duration by several methods. Two are being given here:

- Set a certain count of numbers at a definite rhythm. The rhythm must not vary. Count mentally in each breath. Say, if you feel that your capacity permits only a count up to five at a certain rhythm in each exhalation, then the inhalation also should consist of the same duration
- Instead of numbers, a *mantra* or a prayer word may be used, at the same rhythm consistently

There are other ways of equalising the breath, such as counting the heartbeat or the pulse beat but these would create jerkiness of breath in the beginner.

One needs to observe one's capacity with care. One may find that one can take a breath up to the count of ten, so one becomes enthusiastic and tries to force the same length each time. But after a few breaths, it leads to gasping and jerkiness. Do not force yourself. Establish a mean, according to your capacity.

- Breathe gently, slowly, smoothly and without a jerk. A jerky mind will produce a jerky breath; a jerky breath will generate a jerky mind in return. (Is body the egg and the mind the chicken or is mind the egg and body the chicken — it cannot be said at this stage)
- Observation of the flow and the touch of the breath should be constant, unbroken
- Permit no break, no pause, between the breaths. One who has mastered the pause becomes a master of the forces of time and of death

The pause between the breaths is like a door, outside which a whole crowd of rowdies waits.

Steps in the Subtleties

When the length of breath by a certain count of numbers or *mantra*-remembrances has become easy and natural and requires no effort, then increase the length by a few counts, applying the same principle of 'not forcing' and 'not becoming over-enthusiastic'.

After some time, counting may no longer be necessary. The breath will regulate itself.

At this point, not before, one may begin to experiment with the length of breath in 1:2 ratio, so that if inhalation is to the count of four, the exhalation is to the count of eight.

At first continue to practice equal duration for the major part of the meditation session and use 1:2 ratio to experiment for shorter durations. If one experiences gasps and jerks, then one is not yet ready.

Slowly increase the time for this new practice, and when it becomes easy, eliminate the previous definition of equal duration.

For the elimination of pause, resort to two stratagems:

- Count the breaths (not to be confused with counting within the breath to establish duration). This, again, has three methods:

  * Count exhalation as one; inhalation as two; exhalation three; inhalation four; exhalation five. Next inhalation five; exhalation four; inhalation three; exhalation two; inhalation one. Thus continue one through five and five through one for whatever length of time you can sustain. This is the optimum count during which a beginner's mind remains easily flowing without much extraneous thought

  * Gradually one may experiment by increasing the count to ten: one through to ten; ten through to one

  * When the above has been mastered, one may increase the count to whatever set number one wishes or one may choose to count straight but not backwards — but watch out for the mind wandering away

- Towards the end of each breath, prepare the mind to observe the transition. Observe the transition to the next breath

For deepening the breath awareness, assimilate two more methods:

- As has been said above, do not permit the body to become tense during inhalation, which the body commonly does as a correlate of the activation of the sympathetic nervous system. Keep relaxing; stay relaxed during inhalation

- Pay special attention to exhalation; observe it with a greater depth of the mind

Mastery of the Pause

- The primary outcome of the mastery of the pause is that while this far, one attempted to eliminate the pause, then one enters a state of instantaneous breath-hiatus, which is not to be confused with life-threatening involuntary apnoea. We would also not use the term 'retention' as that may connote inhaling and retaining, as in *abhyantara-kumbhaka*. That is not the intention here. The practice produces a spontaneous attenuation of breath to such a degree that the respiratory process ceases without an anterior or posterior condition. In this state,

- the mind becomes a chamber of silence

- an unprecedented control over the autonomic processes ensues

- finally leading to the first stages of ecstasy (Dr. Feuerstein's term), *samadhi*

- In yoga and respiratory astrology, breath is the basic unit of time. One who has mastered the pause between the breaths becomes a master of the *kala-shakti* forces of time. Alongwith phonetic astrology, it is a secret branch of astrology known only to *yogis*

- Death is a long pause between two breaths, the last breath taken with the current body and the next breath with the next one. One who masters the pause between the breaths becomes a *mrtyunjaya* (death-conqueror). Such a being has learnt the art of longevity. One may postpone one's own death or the death of a beloved disciple who is considered worthy of enhancing the spiritual teaching or advancing to a higher state in this very body. Such a death conqueror sets his own time and place for leaving the body

What is Meditation?

The definition of meditation changes at each step as one traverses to the higher and yet higher ground. The definition in the beginning stages is often repeated in the *Yoga-sutra* study and in the texts such as the *Bhagavad Gita* and the *Brahma-sutras*. It is simply:

- *Samana-pratyaya-pravahah*: the continuous flow of one and the same cognition
- *Anya-pratyaya-anantaritah*: not interrupted by an external cognition

The mind needs an object of concentration. The word 'object' suggests an ontological thing — something external, whereas meditation is an internalised practice. The word 'object' is a poor replacement for the Sanskrit term that is not *vishaya* (object), but *alambana*, any cognition or state that the mind may 'hang on to' internally. 'Hanging on to it', the mind's attention must flow continuously, without interruption. The same *vrtti* (operation) and wave of mind continuing, each following cognition unit is identical to the preceding one. The way a series of points makes a line, so the mind flows in a straight stream.

With human personality, the most easily discernible cognition of flow is that of the breath. The mind has a habit of sculpting itself immediately to the shape and form of whatever 'object' is presented to it. Thus, breath awareness in itself does not constitute meditation. Breath awareness is used to trick the mind into flowing into a state of meditation.

Let the mind be interwoven into the experience of breath awareness, and then the mind begins to flow.

Observation

Observation is an important component in the practice

of meditation. The various components of human personality perform innumerable functions. When we are not aware of them, it is non-meditation. The observation of a function or a process becomes a stage in meditation. For example, we breathe all the time. When we observe the breath flow, it becomes meditation. Thoughts arise at all times; only when we observe them, it becomes part of meditation.

One should not only observe *a process* going on within the personality, and the meditative process itself involved in such observation, but discern whether the function and the process within the personality, and the meditative process is going on correctly and perfectly or incorrectly and imperfectly, and identify as to exactly at what stage of meditation one's consciousness is.

In the *Yoga-sutra* commentaries, this practice is termed *uha*, observing and discerning. In *Yoga of Six Limbs*, shad-anga-yoga of the *tantras*, it is called *tarka*, observation and analysis. It is also an extremely important component in the practice of *anu-smrti*, mindfulness in the *sutras*, and *anussati* in the Buddhist meditative tradition.

The final step before arriving at the *a-manaska-yoga* (no-mind-yoga), where the mind is left behind and only the pure consciousness remains, is the mind observing the mind in its totality.

Presence of a *Mantra*

The presence of a *mantra* replaces the mind's tendency to random sub-vocalisation of thoughts.

Mind Flow and Observation

As we have said above, the breath awareness does not constitute meditation in the strictest sense. As the mind begins to flow, because it is sitting on the banks of the stream of breath, it enters a state of meditation. At this stage observe how the breath, mind and the *mantra* (or your prayer word) flow together as a single stream.

Note the word 'observe'. All manners of operations, functions, activities and experiences go on within the human personality. Because we have condemned ourselves to *mudha*, a permanent comatose state, we do not observe these. As we begin to awaken, we begin to observe these events. It is at the observation point that meditation begins. Hence

- flow of mind on a chosen cognition
- observation of that cognition
- observation of the flow of mind on that cognition

All these constitute meditation at this stage. Once again here, observe how the mind, breath and the *mantra* flow together as a single stream. Become absorbed in this observation, making sure to keep the body relaxed during inhalations, and permitting no pause but observing the transition between the breaths.

For the next level of subtlety, the qualification for which is gained after much intensely concentrated *abhyasa* (endeavour) and *tapas*, ignore the observation of the breath flow; only observe the flow of the mind, and how the entire mind becomes an even-flowing stream.

Here the *alambana* is simply the mind's flow which is to be observed. See how the entire mind becomes an even-flowing stream. Initially an aspirant may not be able to maintain the observation for a duration of more than one or two breaths.

In that case, return to the breath-flow. And, after a while, again try the pure-mind flow observation. Thus practising repeatedly, form the habit of entering the subtlest state known to you easily, even without using a technique; just going directly into that subtle level, anytime, anywhere, while in the midst of all activity. As you practice this uninterrupted mind-flow observation, speak only while in silence, eat only while fasting, meditate in the midst of a riot.

Entering *Sushumna*

When one has reasonably mastered the observation of the even-flowing breath, with the above qualifications, one proceeds to the next stages.

The force in both nostrils becomes equal so that

- neither nostril is active or passive
- both hemispheres of the brain are equally charged or equally pacified, creating a single and totally balanced mind-field. All forces *pinda*, in one's personality, and in, *brahmanda* (the universe), that appeared to be opposite now become complementary and unified
- At this point the feel of the breath flow is not only equally distributed in both nostrils, but appears to the aspirant that the two sides have merged into one. The energy stream is unified. One feels as though the single unified breath is flowing through a central channel
- The concentration then naturally shifts to a central stream. One's attention is drawn to the point in front and centre of the nostrils, *nasagra*. This is a point in front of the septum where the nose bridge joins the upper lip and the wall between the two nostrils begins. It is the final entry and exit point of *sushumna*. This word may be translated as

'purely beautified and harmonised stream in sweet-flowing contemplation'. One inhales as though the energy stream, whose external manifestation is breath, is being inhaled from this point (as in the Tibetan story of Ajogipa, who showed to a disciple 3,000 worlds in a mustard seed placed at this spot) and is being exhaled to this point. The outward-conscious *hatha-yogis* mistakenly think that this point is at the tip of the nose. The *dhyana-yogis* have specifically and emphatically corrected that mistake in order to turn the attention inwards

For a beginner, the experience does not occur without an initiation of that degree.

This path of entry into *sushumna* stream (out of thousand possible paths, such as the *kriya* of spinal breath) is a short cut and in some cases may be opened spontaneously while in many others, it requires the necessary preparations.

Frequent Meditation

Long hours of sitting are not essential. Short, intent meditations practised repeatedly are more conducive for a person leading a busy, mundane life. Try to give yourself two or three intent minutes many times in the day.

- As soon as you open your eyes in bed
- During the bath or shower
- Before breakfast
- Before leaving for work
- After sending the children to school
- Before taking lunch
- Upon coming home from work
- Before leaving for shopping

* After returning from shopping
* Sitting in the car before driving out
* Stopping the car a few blocks away before arriving at a party
* Before a job interview
* Before taking a business, family or personal decision
* Sitting in the Board of Directors meeting while others are arguing
* During an examination when the mind goes blank
* While waiting for the taxi
* While standing in the queue to pay at the supermarket
* While waiting at the airport security or departure gate
* Before giving in to a surge of emotion
* During the two-minute commercial breaks in the TV programmes
* While falling asleep

The list is not exhaustive. Not having time is no excuse. These segments of time are always available to one. The mind always has plenty of time, depending on what you have chosen for the mind to do with that ever-available time.

Sleep Transitions
Another subtlety may be introduced to make one's life harmonious with a meditative stance. Do not go to sleep

* from wakefulness
* through reveries and fantasies
* through a period of tossing and turning
* through meditation
* from the awake state to meditation to sleep

* in the morning
* from sleep, direct into meditation
* to wakefulness

New Habit, Next Plateau

Whatever the mind does repeatedly will become its habit, and then its nature. Because we maintain the disturbed states repeatedly, they become the mind's habitual states.

If the mind is calmed repeatedly through the above practices, calmness will become its natural state. From that plateau of initial achievement one begins the climb to a higher one, till the consciousness has totally entered singularity in infinity.

* Nothing short of infinity will do
* Be ambitious

CHAPTER 2

GROUP MEDITATION

THE UNIVERSAL MIND

We increase our count of pleasures by always adding subtler pleasures to ourselves. One of the subtler pleasures is to be silently associated with a group. People often ask me, "Can I not sit and meditate in my own little home on my meditation seat and not come to a group?" Others ask me, "Well, I do better if I have group support." The ideal is to transcend the need for group support, but that ideal is like the ideal of final enlightenment.

Group meditation can be of three kinds: meeting at the same place and time; meeting at the same place but not necessarily at the same time; meeting at the same time but not at the same place. Let's look at it all in detail. We need to understand how the yoga tradition defines the mind.

In the yoga tradition, as I have said many times before, the individual mind — though an important entity — is not the only mind. The primary mind is the universal mind. Here I'm very careful about using my terms because when I say universal mind, I do not mean God; I mean the 'mind'. In the universal mind, like whirls in the sea, there are fields and sub-fields that are perpetually present or those that can be generated. When we all meditate together, a force-field is created among the meditating minds. That force-field gradually and slowly helps to uplift you from your individuated ego because you may transcend from your individual mind to the next step, towards realising the entity called the universal mind.

We experience this field, a common mental field, when we have a harmonious family. That is one way in which we all transcend our personal egos and many become as one. In a spiritual family, we do not need to have interaction, not primarily on the vocal level, but on the silent level of a meditating group. The experience of group meditation then becomes the experience of this newly-generated or ancient-one, awakened, force-field, common force-field, of all the people who meditate together. It becomes a stepping stone towards the realisation of the entity called the universal mind into which we then slowly, gradually, ascend upwards, learning to surrender our tiny egos so that we may become larger.

Meditating at the same place but not at the same time is simply this: where the *guru* has meditated; where those who were made one with the universal mind have meditated; where saints have dwelled; places where nothing has ever happened except prayer. And in a meditation centre which is set aside for the purpose of meditation alone, a force-field is created. And when one individual person comes to meditate there, he joins his individual mind entity to that universal force-field and is thereby uplifted, elevated, pacified, made calm and energised. A minor or a major miracle can happen there. A person may be mentally healed. A person may even be physically healed, depending on the strength of the force-field present. These are miraculous places.

Each meditation centre can create a minor miracle by having such a force-field in the place where people meditate together.

When a group meditates at the same time, some members — one, two, three, or four, or five — may join together and say, let us give each other quiet, mental support. Let us meditate at the same time in our home. So, let us say we shall meditate at 5:30 in the morning. If it's a silent and quiet understanding with a resolve, then somehow the persons involved will begin to wake up at the right time every day. There will be an urge over a period of time not to miss that connection. In fact, if one person out of this group of five misses his meditation seat at that time, or misses the time of being present at the meditation seat, quite often it is likely that others in the group will know and will call up and ask if everything is alright. If a person is ill, he may do so — join the group — even while lying in bed.

Many times, people ask, "How can we send healing energies to others?" Until we have been granted the grace and power to do so, we can do it by including others in our commonly-generated meditation force-field. That is, five people meditating together may help to heal each other. They don't need to do anything special for that healing. Simply the fact that a force-field is being generated is sufficient. Over a period of time, your energy grows, your mind becomes laser sharp, and then you can beam the power. But it will not happen by fanciful imagination. It is a very specific thing which one needs to learn at a later time. But what will happen with many people meditating at the same time but in different places, is that if one person misses, others will know. It's not an invasion of privacy. It is an engulfing through love. I wish you this healing of minds, healing of bodies, elevating of yourselves from the littlenesses of ego identification to the vast universal mind through a gradual ascent up the ladder of quietude, through a gradual dive into the depths of the calmest part of the sea called the 'mind'.

Now, as you are, where you are, sit; sit gently. Do nothing. Make no effort. Abandon all endeavours of the body and mind. Relax. Go through no method, no technique. Simply, wherever you have ever been deepest in the quietness of the mind, whatever the deepest you have ever experienced of the gentleness and stilling of the mind, go there directly. Go there and sit as long as you wish. I will sit with you at a different place but at the same time now. Go there and sit within for as long as you wish. God bless you.

CHAPTER 3

DIFFERENT KINDS OF ADVANCED MEDITATION

THE SYNTHESIS OF *SANDHYA* AND CENTRED BREATH

The main element of celibacy and the practices relating to it are meant to develop the inward flow. As I have said in my earlier lectures on the *chakras*, 'opening means closing' — closing the outward doors of the energies that we fritter away, and opening the inward gates so that the energies may be absorbed, when assimilated into our personalities and become the vehicles of the ascent of our consciousness to the highest divine pedestal within us.

After having understood the basic breathing processes of yoga and meditation, the role of *kundalini* and the role of the *chakras* in it, the practice of *sushumna* (breathing) is one of the subtlest methods for centring the consciousness. There is *sushumna* breathing in the spine, or there is the upper *sushumna* breath, that is between the *ajna chakra* (the 'third-eye' centre) and the point where the 'nose-bridge' joins the upper lip. This crucial point is known as *nasagre* or *nasagra* and has been specifically defined as "the point between the two nostrils where the base of the nose joins the upper lip." Concentration on this point can result in the manifestation of *gandha-pravrtti* (celestial smells). The meditation teacher can teach this breathing process if you have not learned so far.

Here let me say one thing. Gender is a projection. Within you there are both genders physically. Doctors will tell you that everyone is first formed as a female in the early stages of the foetus, so the female remains in us even though we may be males. Something of the male remains in the female — the male hormones that exist in females. Those that are known as female hormones exist in males. The left-nostril breath and the right-nostril breath constitute a wedded couple. The left hemisphere of the brain and the right hemisphere of the brain form a complete whole. What is tangibly manifest in us also conceals that which is intangible, unmanifested, lying somewhat concealed, over-powered by the partiality of the mind, the body bias, which has many psycho-physiological dimensions.

Merging the 'left' and the 'right' within us leads us to that central channelling becoming *madhya-stha* (middle-centred, middle-staying), channelling in the centre, whereby the opposite principles merge into one and are experienced as a single stream of consciousness. That is the essence of celibacy: the merger of the two into one central channel so that there is nothing to contrast. Then there are no opposites; thus we are not bound by one type of body bias and feeling incomplete in that or projecting the other unmanifest part on to others and seeing them as the *other* gender. In other words, all gender attraction in a very deep, subtle manner is a form of narcissism. That which is within me I do not clearly see because of my partiality, my particular body bias and my mind bias, and yet I long for it — for that which is within me — and I want to love it. I cannot find it quite clearly, so I project it on to others, and in them I love this *other* part of me, and thereby hope to make myself complete. It is a convoluted way to make oneself complete. Only those who are experts at *tantra*, which I have defined as 'the art and science of celibacy', can be quite successful in this central channelling, as this central channelling is discovered by them together. But that is a different topic.

THE ROOT LOCK

There are other practices also. Just as to effect the silence of speech in the *mantra*-remembrance process, we turn the tongue into the palate and lock it away so that the mental sensation does not become lingual, we also close off other avenues through which our energies flow outwards. For example, one practices *mula-bandha*, translated as the 'root-lock'. To understand this you will need to listen to the lectures on the first *chakra*. The root-lock is not simply the pulling of the outer muscles of the buttocks but it should be felt at the level of the sphincter. If it feels like a distraction during meditation, then it may be abandoned until such time as it becomes natural. To make it natural, one tries to practice maintaining the root-lock at all times. For success in maintaining the root-lock, the other practice is *ashvini mudra*. In *ashvini mudra* one contracts the sphincter as much as one can, then relaxes the sphincter — and continues in this way as long as one can, till the root-lock automatically forms. One who is accomplished in *ashvini mudra* and the root-lock can be a perfect celibate. When our *gurudev*, Swami Rama, performs *mula-bandha*, his hips shrink and practically become non-existent; he pulls from all the surrounding muscles.

KEVALA AND *KAIVALYA* — 'GOING SOLO'

The *Oxford English Dictionary* says that the word 'celibacy' is directly related to the Sanskrit word *kevala* (solo). Celibacy is the practice of being 'solo'. Not physically 'solo', not making oneself suffer loneliness, but rather having oneself enjoy solitude. Solitude here, in relation to celibacy, does not necessarily mean locking oneself in a monastic cell. It is to progress towards that desirable state where the soul is solo, where it has divorced, abandoned, left behind the force called *maya* or *prakriti* (matter, exterior Nature) and is aware of itself being the non-dependent spirit. 'Being solo' means declaring the spirit's independence, its non-dependence on matter. It is the last word in the *Yoga-sutras* — *kaivalya*, ultimate solitude, the goal of yoga. This can be accomplished only through a sense of internal freedom. There is a word in the *Vedas* — *svarajyam* (self-conquest). It is the state of renunciation; a state of being so full of freedom within that one is a joy within oneself — so filled with the power that one has immense riches to give and distribute in an inexhaustible way. One becomes capable of giving unconditional love, which requires no reciprocity, which looks for no reciprocity, in which the question of reciprocity does not arise — because reciprocity is always from the *other*, and there is no *other* there. It is the soul's own *solo* Nature-in-God from which love flows; and whoever comes in your presence goes away feeling loved in a very pure non-physical way — his mind filled by you; his heart fulfilled without requiring any physical pretexts for feeling that.

RECONDITIONING ONE'S ATTITUDES TOWARDS GENDER ROLES

Now let's take a different attitude. We have to take these attitudes one by one. It will take a long time to cultivate them, to recondition your emotionality, to recondition your sentimentality, to redefine your meaning of sentiment. In the cultures that value premarital celibacy, there is a particular attitude towards inter-gender relationships. It says — take this fictitious thing called man, this fictitious thing called woman. There are *four* in each of these. In man there is a father; there is a brother; there is a son; and there is a male. So only one-quarter is male, and the other three-quarters are something other than overt gender. Some gender-engendered qualities recognised in a non-gender way make one a father, a brother, or a son. In this fictitious entity of a woman, there is a mother, a sister, a daughter, and one-quarter is female. The status of a mother, sister and daughter is three times larger than the status of relationship in the male-female terminology. Similarly, the status as a father, brother, or son is three times larger. And that is why in Western countries, if one meets an elderly lady, she is addressed as 'Auntie'. She is not your aunt but you call her Auntie. Sometimes you address a completely strange woman as 'Sister'. In a country like India where the training of emotions and emotional responses is very, very different, (except perhaps for the recent 20 per cent in the upper class, English-speaking, urban population which is exposed to international TV — a tragedy unfolding in 80 per cent of the rest of the population — I do not know for how many generations this form of respect will continue). Any woman older than oneself is addressed as 'Ma,' or 'Mataji.' Someone of your sister's age — anywhere, any place — a complete stranger is addressed in the same term we use for our sister, elder sister: *Didi, Bahan*. Any girl who would be of daughter's age would be addressed as *Beti*, my daughter, my child. And similarly the other way around with males: women addressing males the same way, give them the status of a father, brother, son.

There is an old joke that came from the 1950's when I was still learning English by reading the wonderful *Reader's Digest*. A person asked, "If a woman and two men were stranded on a desert island, what would happen?" Well, you know the national stereotypes. It said, if they are French, then there is no problem. If they are Italians, one man will kill the other and marry the woman. If they are Spanish, the woman will kill one of the men and marry the other. And if they are British, well, nothing will happen because they haven't been introduced. Excuse me, as French or Italian or Spanish or British were mentioned, I felt discriminated against because they didn't say what would happen if they were from India. But I'll tell you what would happen — the woman would adopt one as a brother who will give her away as a bride to the other man. It is still very common, whether you are married or a young teenager in our society in which sexual relationships are taken very seriously. I remember talking about this in Calgary a number of years ago, when I said I have 'a sister in every port.' Those who have been sisterly to me, before taking my vows, I maintained that relationship with them. Now my relationship as a *swami* is slightly changed. But in this way, whether we are congenitally related or not, we establish the fatherly-motherly, brotherly-sisterly, daughter-son, filial relationships. So that instead of viewing others as males and females with that gender superimposed on them, we accept our congenital father, brother, son; accept our congenital mother, sister, daughter, instead of making it the other way round. Every male is father-brother-son except that one we are married to, or would marry. Every woman is mother-sister-daughter, except the one we marry. And this gives a sense of fulfilment without the emotional and physical involvements of the kind that are inter-gender. So, let the three-fourths absorb the one-fourth. That is celibacy at the level of emotional and sentimental relationships.

VAIRAGYA: THE ART OF EMOTIONAL NEUTRALITY

I have been asked at times since I have been a *swami* and before "you travel around so much and interact with so many people" that some people hoped that I would have some salacious confessions to make, but I have none. And they ask me, "How do you manage that, because there must be times when people in your congregation are attracted to you in a non-priestly way?" Yes, it is true. I simply do not acknowledge the approach. I carry on as I am. I do not get repulsed. I do not get attracted. I do not run away. I do not show revulsion. I do not show horror. I do not shut the other person out. I do nothing. I just do nothing mentally. Neither does my mental state change, nor my voice, nor my body language in any way. And I continue to behave with the person as one should behave with one's initiate, and after a while that mood in the other person just wears off. In *Sutra 15* of the first chapter in the *Yoga-sutras*, four levels of dispassion are described. Defined in the *Yoga-sutras* as "the state of being devoid of, free from *raga*, the attraction that accrues from objects of attraction reflecting in and colouring the mind." These are *yatamana* (the initial effort), *vyatireka* (ascertainment and analysis on one's progress), *ekendriya* (working on those attractions that dwell only in the mind), and *vashikara* (control and mastery). The word *ekendriya* literally means 'one sense only'. That is, when the exterior senses cease reacting to the stimuli but some memories, some *samskaras* (impressions) still arise in the mind, there is no inclination to indulge physically even though the opportunity presents itself. It is like the state of married persons who are in love with each other — it does not mean they do not recognise that someone else is attractive, but there is no inclination to indulge in pursuing that attractiveness. Marriage, therefore, is a form of celibacy by exclusion — excluding all the others but this one person. Final celibacy excludes even that.

THE JOY OF ABSTINENCE

When one learns to conserve one's energies — not by suppression, but by attitude and awakening of the centres of consciousness and breathing practices — and the sensuality is merged with the supreme and the sublime, the energies that one earlier frittered away become assimilated. And do you know what happens? Two things happen — all the body sensations become more intense. It seems that you become a powerhouse of sensuality, and there is a strong temptation to expend it; and if you do not know how to absorb it, you may become restless. You will see more clearly; hear more sharply. You will taste flavours you have not tasted before in the same food that you are used to. Your skin will respond, as well as everything else in your body. If you understand what is happening, observe it and rejoice that you are becoming intense, that you are becoming a powerhouse, that you are becoming a magnet — the same magnetism some day will be used for initiating others into spirituality. Your speech will become effective because of this concealed power behind it. Together with that, you would become more charming and more attractive. People are drawn to you, not knowing what they are drawn to — and this is the undoing of many a celibate. I have seen this tragedy happen. The innocence of a flower is such that our hands are naturally drawn to pluck it before the flower knows that it is being plucked. Whenever I think of sending young men, who are trained in the *ashram* tradition and who have been celibate, to Western countries, there is always this innate fear that they will be plucked because of their charm, because of their attractiveness, because of their magnetism. And by touching that flower, by running your finger on its innocent petals, you destroy it. If, however, you create a society in which innocence is honoured and respected, the way you honour your daughter's body and protect it, in the way that you dedicate a society to a behaviour in which people's emotions and sentiments are trained to venerate the untouched, unplucked flower, then, you will have a society in which males and females will be virgins at marriage. And such a thing is a gift: to preserve oneself for "*that* one to whom I shall give myself." And such a sentiment is developed by all these other cultural, familial and supporting systems. Then the celibates will also be protected and people would only touch their feet and seek their blessing.

So absorb, assimilate and intensify internally.

PSYCHO-PHYSIOLOGICAL RHYTHMS

Everyone has noticed that at certain times a desire arises intensely. That moment, if fully understood, can contribute to your mastery of the senses. You have to understand the moment of the rising of desire in terms of your diurnal rhythms. For example, sleep has its own rhythms. It is known that in many dreams, both in males and females, the occurrence of tumescence is common. And when the dream part of the rhythm passes, the tumescence subsides. In daytime also, the brain maintains a similar rhythm. This rhythm in sleep or wakefulness is not only seen in the form of neurons firing, but also in the alteration of breath rhythms.

Be a *neutral* observer of your body. Long ago I gave a course on 'desire', the origin of desire, the meaning of desire, etc., and I said that one should learn to postpone the indulgence in desires — 'okay, not now; later' — and then that part of the rhythm passes and ceases to be such a reality. That is one practice.

Secondly, when the sensuality is at its most intense, *that* is the time to meditate; *that* is the time to channelise it; to absorb it; it is there — manifest. Get into meditation, and the desire that makes you want to fritter away your energy outwards will turn inwards, and the flow of the *sushumna* stream will be *so* clear, *so* sharp, that it will lead you to a completely different kind of serene ecstasy. And you will have absorbed the power, as though a few more coils were being added to the electro-magnet to enhance its power. When you will arise from such a meditation, your creativity will be at its most fruitful. You will *never* feel a blockage — if you are a writer, a poet, or a painter — if you know how to enhance, how to absorb, how to assimilate, how to channelise, and how to use it creatively. Your pure love will be effective. Your speech will be effective. Your smiles will charm the most avowed enemy. And you will not walk — if you have learned *mula-bandha* and *ashvini mudra* and you have absorbed the energy — you will prance like a deer; you will prance like a doe as though you have springs in your feet. If you spend a month of celibacy in total silence and *japa*, as I have taught in the 'Silence' series in 1995, people will see a light on your face. That light has a special term — it is called *Brahma-tejas*. Quite often we hear people referring to a teacher or a *swami* as someone whose face has *Brahma-tejas*, a divine light, a halo, visible to those who have eyes to see. And that light will lighten others' minds, others' spirits without their knowing it. And it will be efficacious in your path of service. When you have power, use it for serving. Use it altruistically, and keep gathering more, so that you may give more, so that you may initiate more people by your glance, by your touch, by your word. I do not mean here just giving a *mantra* initiation. It is a power whereby you throw a spiritual mantle, and they sit listening. Their mind becomes a chamber in pin-drop silence. Look for these subtle gifts.

TRUE INTIMACY

For the married ones, I would like to suggest that you be aware of a 'morning-after effect'. See what your mood is after a night of celibacy in which you have loved each other in a spiritual way, in which you have been able to synchronise your breathing, so that when the left nostril of one partner flows, the right nostril of the other partner too flows. Although this is not the topic here, there are *tantric* techniques whereby you can share your energies, and see the morning-after effect of such a celibate night of sharing love. You would be surprised at the intensity of non-physical love that is so very fulfilling. The ability for silent communication will be enhanced. Since all your senses will sharpen, you will see in your partner what you have not seen before. You will discover beauty that you did not know existed. You will enjoy the cadences of the voice more. You will listen to them, and they will become a symphony. The art of marital love is closely tied to the art of celibacy.

One word more on marital regularity — reduction of frequency of indulgence will not only give you these spiritual benefits, it will also intensify the pleasure of indulgence when you *do* express your love that way.

The Sanskrit word for celibacy is *Brahmacharya* ('walking in God'), dwelling in God, living in God, becoming solo.

For those who are serious about their celibacy, they cannot do it without prayer; they cannot do it without grace. I have spoken in my lectures on the *chakras* about the principle of 'push' and 'pull'. The lower energies 'push' the energies up; the higher *chakras* 'pull' the energies up. One who has reconditioned oneself, who has retrained one's emotions and sentiments and responses to sensuality, one who has learned to observe it neutrally and apply it for his or her spiritual enhancement, he will find that the moment some sensation triggers a desire, or an inclination triggers a sensation in a certain region of the body commonly associated with gender, this sensation will immediately go to the *ajna chakra* (third eye). Practice concentrating at the point between the eyebrows, thinking that the sex force is being drawn up to the brain, where it can be used for mental and spiritual purposes. The life energy is the very instrument with which you work for spiritual awakening. It is the fund you have saved in the bank. If you spend it, dissipate it in excessive sexual pleasure, you will have no strength to fight for the higher life. But if you will save it, hoard it, and lead it upward to the brain, you may use it for creative work and for self-realisation — a thrilling thought, a glorious possibility. This sensation exists only to remind oneself that here is this powerhouse, this storehouse of energy. "Let it flow through the wires up to the right place" — and through that gate of the 'third eye', you will enter the depths of the mind. And beyond the 'third eye', there is the *guru chakra* which will link you to the lineage of the saints. The more intense the desire is the sharper the beam of energy will be to cut through the darkness in the mind and take you to the central core where the light of spirit resides — unpollutable, incorruptible, unchangeable, indomitable, invincible. In *tantra*, it is referred to as the *bindu-rakshana*. *Bindu* is that point in the mind into which all energies are absorbed and from which they emanate — the point of the

centripetal and centrifugal forces of the mind — that from which
the power of the faculties emanates, radiates, and into which it
is re-absorbed. When your prayer or your *mantra* becomes one-
pointed, the single point of the mind, so that the mind is no
longer thought of as being separate from this particular prayer-
point — preserving *that* 'drop', preserving *that* point, is the
preservation of celibacy. Do not let the 'drop' scatter. When you
have thus preserved the 'drop' and maintained the point, then
comes the next step, and that is called *bindu-bhedan* (bursting,
piercing through the point) — going to a higher level. But what
I suggest is, if you are spiritually also serious, just as you take
retreats sometimes and go away, take retreats from sensuality for
short periods. Give yourself short periods of abstinence, but you
cannot do it without prayer or without *japa*. Celibacy of the body
is difficult without celibacy of the mind. The *Bhagavad Gita* says,
"There are many who cease indulging in the physical senses but
keep dwelling on thoughts." The true accomplishment is when
you can practice a period of silence in which you have said, 'My
thoughts shall be celibate.' What do you do with your thoughts?
Well, you channelise them elsewhere. That is where your prayer
and your *japa* comes in. And if you can do this, the light that will
be seen on your face will be the topic of many an artist's painting
for centuries to come — for this is the true transformation; this
is the true ascension to heavenly consciousness.

I feel very sorry, very sad, for those who have a strong tradition
of celibacy in priesthood but have not been taught its meaning,
or that it is an enhancing experience and have to suffer it as a
denial. I have seen many a forced celibate towards the later years
of his or her life becoming crotchety and ill-tempered. There is
no shortage of overly-aggressive, bad-tempered monks and nuns

in any religion of the world — those for whom this undertaking is a struggle, a conflict that cannot be resolved, because what I have explained to you here and elsewhere has not been opened to them. And then they want to throw away the opportunity to be celibate and protest against such a blessing. Those of you who on listening to this can come to an understanding of it and want to make tiny, little toddler's steps towards it — not a leap into the sky all at once, through purification of the mind and mental reconditioning, through a new look at one's relationships and sentiments and who have an intense longing for spiritual purification and for meeting my great lover, God, in solitude — 'solo' — to those who will practice this, I wish you success and whatever blessing the spiritual lineage of the Himalayan saints can channelise towards you. May those blessings help you to succeed in your endeavour.

Let these last few words linger in your mind.

COMMON MEDITATION PRACTICES IN OTHER RELIGIONS

We collectively need to find strength in wisdom and its applications that brought about beauty in the past periods of human experience.

We also need to look for examples of some of the common principles and practices in the various religions while recognising some of their fundamental differences as well. We touch upon some of the mistakes that have been made in identifying religions with ethnicities, nations and states and other mundane interests.

We suggest that those who are pursuing the search for unity and harmony among religions need to look into the contemplative paths and meditative traditions.

In that we

- briefly explore some of these methodologies of meditation that are held in common among religions
- suggest that the internal peace of the individual mind generated through meditational pursuits and practices is a prerequisite for establishing peace in the societies

One need not be a believer to practice meditation to receive its benefits by way of an internal calm that it generates. There are meditation methods equally valid for non-believers — the efficacy of which has been proved in scientific and medical investigations in the last five decades.

Education for peace will begin when training the mind to calmness through meditation methodologies becomes part of the educational system without prejudice to anyone's belief in a religious doctrine or in absence thereof.

May human beings learn to remember what has been harmonious and beautiful in the past and may they recognise what is right in the present.

MEDITATION: THE UNIFYING STREAM IN RELIGION

The quest for unity among religions is an ancient one that continues to this day. A history of the successes of such quest will take a large volume to define and describe. Some of the many examples of such successes, and how they were achieved, may be mentioned here by way of illustration:

- Through reinterpretation. For example, the reinterpretation of the Old Testament to absorb the Jewish ideas into Christianity but with a different meaning
- Through discussion among the leaders of various religions. For example, an inter-religious conference among Hinduism, Buddhism, and so on, to give a cohesive form to the best elements among these religions
- Through absorption of ideas, belief systems and practices of an earlier religion on to a later one

The examples of this abound in history, such as (a) Christmas tree absorbed into Christianity, (b) the Hindu symbols and emblems in Thai Buddhism, (c) the Hindu legends and rituals absorbed into the Malay (both Indonesian and Malaysian) Islam,

(d) the Inca and Aztec deities absorbed as saint figures in South American Christianity, (e) the contemporary experiments in Africa to absorb the divine, celestial, saintly, or prophetic figures of the African tradition into the new churches and religions, (f) Hindu songs sung with themes around Rama and Krishna and adapted to the Muslim sentiment on occasions like Muharram or in the *qawwalis.*

- Through mutual exchange of ideas, and an accommodation in the community, where there are parallels in the practices derived from different sources to enrich the lives of the individuals and societies. For example, the successful exchanges that occurred among Taoism, Confucianism and Buddhism in China and Korea; among Taoism, Confucianism, Shintoism and Buddhism in Japan; Hindu practices in South Asian Islam; Muslim and Christian practices in contemporary Hinduism of many varieties

- Through understanding among neighbouring individuals and societies out of respect for each other, for example, Hindus distributing sweets to Muslims and vice versa on the celebration of Eid, and Muslims giving out sweets on occasions like Diwali

- Through reverence for sanctity, which is innate and almost instinctive, wherever it may be found. For example, the Hindus worshipping at the *dargahs* of the Muslim saints

- Many other such processes of the development of mutual co-existence and absorption need to be researched in the entire world history, recognising the fact that these did not take place out of fear but from a natural human urge towards amity and reverence

One of the strongest bonds of unity among religions occurs

when the contemplators of various streams compare notes of the experience of divine silence where all doctrinal verbosity ceases and only an interior and all-engulfing peace prevails.

The archetypes in the universal consciousness manifest themselves in numerous identical ways and forms in all religious traditions. Again, a few examples of these parallel experiences may be cited here:

- All religions have towering prophetic figures as their founders. These may be individual founders of a religion, for example Zarathushtra, the founder of the Mazdayasnians and Hazrat Mohammad, the founder of Islam. Groups of founders, for example,
  - lineages of *rishis* and *avatars* (divine incarnations) in Hinduism
  - the prophets of the Jewish lineage such as Abraham, Moses, and their descendants
  - the Tirthankaras of the Jaina tradition
  - the chain of Buddhas in both the northern and southern versions of Buddhism
  - the ten *gurus* of the Sikh faith. The tradition of reading and reciting the lives of the founders and the great sages of the religion
- The fact of each religion's faith in the processes of divine revelations and the resulting sacred books
- Sacred words, phrases, sentences, verses or texts, which may be memorised and recited repeatedly
- Sacred spaces and waters, be they natural phenomena such as mountains, holy rivers and streams or special edifices
- Sacred music and chant

- Prayer and liturgies. The forms and wording may differ, but the fact of prayer remains, even in religions that do not believe in a Creator or God
- Different body positions for prayer, such as sitting in a certain way or kneeling or standing with hands clasped or the hands open to heaven
- The *mudras*, the gestures and positions of the face, hands and body parts as manifest in the divine and sacred figures
- The importance of the divine name. One begins 'with the name of Allah', or in the Zarathushtrian tradition, '*Pa name-e-yazdan Hormazd*', or 'in the name of God, Son and Holy Ghost' — the practice of starting a letter, a book or any endeavour by writing the name of God; the exhortations to remember the name of God in every breath, glorifying the name of God, or of a divine figure where no Creator is accepted in stories, legends, rituals, songs, and prayers
- Sanctity of the transitions in
  * life-cycles
  * annual cycles, observed and celebrated through sacraments. Many of these sacraments celebrate identical transitions, such as birth, baptism, Jewish *bar mitzvah* or Vedic *upanayana*, confirmation, marriage, funeral, and so forth; the celebration of seasonal cycles, sacred months and sacred days in the annual cycle
- Dietary laws
  * Prohibition on killing certain animals, either because they pollute or because they are sacred
  * Meatless days whether as
    ‣ a belief in the sanctity of universal life force
    ‣ a presence of soul in all bodies

- ▶ or simply as an act of penitence, self-control or asceticism
- Sanctity of marriage
- Fasting, in varying degrees
- Practice of celibacy, if not as a permanent vow, then during certain times of the life cycle and the annual cycle, for example,
  - exhortations to the practice of *Brahmacharya* in the Vedic tradition until marriage
  - celibacy during certain nights of the month
  - celibacy for monks and priests in various traditions
  - prohibition on being *ham-bistar* during the holy month of Ramzan, and so forth
- Disciplines of clothing, for example, special habits or forms of garments for priests and monks, or covering the head for lay women and nuns in certain Catholic traditions, or taking off the hat or shoes as a mark of reverence for the sacred ground, or other rules of modesty of clothing in the church, temple and mosque
- Priestly orders, monastic orders
- Stories of temptation and the conquest thereof. Examples are the temptation of Nachiketa in the Vedic tradition; of Zarathushtra after ten years in his cave; of the Buddha during forty-nine days under the Bodhi tree; of Jesus after the forty days of seclusion; and the story of Shiva's cosmic temptation by Kamadeva, God of desire, during the former's perennial *samadhi*, and the burning of Kamadeva to ashes through the beam of light emanating from Shiva's third eye
- Period of seclusion, again, for forty days of special spiritual

endeavours, such as practices of prayer, penitence, and self-purification. For example, forty days of Lent; forty days of spring celebrations in India; forty days of *chilla*, the Sufi practice of withdrawing into a place of solitude for intense and incessant ascetic effort, be it in a *chilla-khana*, a cave, a forest or desert hermitage or at any other solitary place

- Belief in a future redeemer
  - the return of the founder of one's own religion as in the case of Jesus
  - any other *Messiah* as in the Jewish tradition
  - the future Buddha like Maitreya in the Buddhist tradition
  - the Kalki *avatar*, the divine incarnation-to-be in Hinduism
- Belief in the transformation of the earthly existence or the earthly city into a heavenly one, such as Jerusalem, Kashi, Go-loka
- Exhortations and commandments to conquer human weaknesses, such as that of anger, jealousy, malice, violence, greed; conquest of desires; principles of ethics based on such exhortations of self-conquest; within that context, the conquest of flesh in all forms
- Similarities of rules for various monastic, celibate or virginal orders, such as the rules for the virgins, the virgin guides of the community in American Indian traditions like the Oneida, or in the African *voodoo* and other sacred traditions, or the institution of Kumari in Hinduism, especially so in Nepal; the similarity of rules of St. Benedict to the earlier rules for monks in the Buddhist, and yet more ancient, the Vedic renunciation orders of *swamis*
- The crucial belief that the human being exists to elevate

himself through great diligence towards spiritual liberation and heavenly consciousness

These are only a few of the examples of the parallels that exist among all religions whether revealed independently of each other, or through a mutual borrowing, or accommodation due to a spiritual urge or co-existence.

All of these areas require a vast undertaking of research so that in the contemporary society, while facing its problems, we may learn from the history of 'what has been right with the world'.

This is not to support the futile statements, such as, all religions are one. In spite of the fact of these similarities cited above, the various streams of religions maintain their own doctrinal systems, which do not agree in major areas of the worldview or the vision and perception of the divine. We may divide humanity's religious experience into at least four major streams:

- Zarathushtrian, which has loaned many fundamental ideas to all the religions of the world
- The Abrahamic religions, that is Jewish, Christian and Islam
- The Indian religions, the Vedic-Tamil-Hindu, Buddhist, Jaina, Santa-mata, Sikh tradition, and numerous others
- Indigenous religions on all continents often dismissed as animistic or Nature religions, because the depth of their philosophy has not been understood. This is simply due to the fact that their followers are economically disadvantaged and not articulate in the modern terminologies of the dominant religions. From Australia, through Africa, through all of the Americas, there runs a common stream of deep

reverence for the presence of the divine in all phenomena. This expresses itself in an unaccountable variety of beliefs, doctrines, songs, stories, epics, rituals and daily undertakings and interactions

The Abrahamic religions may differ from each other on important points of the doctrine and yet they share a certain worldview among themselves. So also do the Indian religions, as well as the various indigenous religions.

When we look at the parallels and similarities, as well as the historical experience of peaceful co-existence in vast areas of human history, we are puzzled as to why there is such dissension and violence of thought (thought first), word and deed among the adherents of these faiths. A close look at the universal phenomena shows us that only a very subtle, slim line separates the positive from the negative, or prevents the positive energies from flowing into negative directions. Thus, distortions occur in the original message of love, tolerance and peace. Some of the examples of these distortions may be given as follows:

- Faith may turn into a frenzy of devotion, manifesting itself in ecstatic song or dance or, on the other hand, into a fury of fanaticism

- In almost all religions, we read passages like, 'I am saviour'. These passages are written in languages where the definitive article 'the' is not known. This is one single word that has caused an immeasurable amount of strife and suffering. We fail to reconcile the saying of Jesus, 'I am Way', with Krishna's statement 'I am Way'. We fail to imagine that the same God has spoken through different embodiments of His own at different time periods, to different ones of His chosen people

Thus mixing the human weaknesses of anger, narrowness and intolerance with the readings of scripture, the adherents of each faith misinterpret the scripture as an exhortation for exclusivity.

- Often the scriptures are not read in the original but as translations, sometimes even of translations; thus an original church member does not know what was the original intent of the words of Jesus in Aramaic translated into Hebrew or Greek or Latin or 16th century English or 21st century American. How many layers of obscuring dust we have laid upon the original meaning! Very easily our mental association with a word like 'apocalyptic' suggests that the *Book of Apocalypse* has to do with a destructive process rather than of the removal of a veil or unveiling, which is the original intent

- As a religion spreads, in spite of its attempt to claim purity, it picks up the ideas and thoughts originally held by the people who are now becoming converts. Often it enriches the religion as
  - the Tamil tradition enriched the Hindu thought of the Vedic origin
  - as did the Balinese traditions enrich the same
  - the Celts and the Druids and the Nordics enriched Christianity
  - the Persian tradition enriched Islam

- Some of the prejudices of those original cultures also creep in and eclipse the original meaning. It is like different people claiming to be racially pure, but none are proved to be so upon examination of their genetic inheritance. It is now no longer possible to eradicate the genes inherited from the millennia of racial mix, so it is not possible to separate the original from the accretions in any religion. The efforts at doing so are not only self-defeating, they are also destructive as, for example, the attempts of some elements of contemporary Islam to 'purify' the Malayan and Indonesian Islam by eliminating all that was preserved in the original cultures

- Often religions have become identified with ethnic groups and nations. One group of people, say in an African territory, accepts the tenets of Islam and another group accepts Christianity. The two are traditional enemies who have perpetrated acts of cruelty, upon the other. Now that cruelty becomes attributed to the religion that they have recently adopted, so it is perceived that the Christians are killing the Muslims or the Muslims are killing the Christians. Actually it is one tribal-minded group killing another tribal-minded group that now happens to have adopted a different religion

- Often the strife among nations manifests itself as an attack on the religion of the defeated and the weaker. An event of this nature that may have occurred twenty or fourteen centuries ago is viewed by us today as an act of religious persecution where as it is, by and large, a conqueror's attempt to destroy the identity of a certain people. An example may be given of Alexander destroying the Zarathushtrian fire temples and burning their holy books. Could the *guru* of Alexander of Macedonia, Aristotle the philosopher, have actually ordered his disciple to destroy such great works of philosophy as the *Gathas* and the *Avesta* of the Mazdayasnians? Yet, the fact of destruction remains, the main purpose of which was the political subjugation of a nation by destroying its identity. This is easily achieved through the desecration and suppression of its religion

- The propagandists of different religions have an age-old habit of
  * choosing the best and most inspiring passages from their own texts
  * the most creative and beautiful periods of their history
  * choosing the worst passages and periods of history from the adherents of an opposite religion and compare the two. In return, those they oppose use the same tool, citing the best examples from their own scripture and history and attacking those of their own opponents. Why not confess to ourselves of our own failures and expunge from our consciousness all that is destructive in our own understanding of the doctrine as well as our own history?
- The age-old enmities among nations, easily identified with the religions that they follow, cultivate and perpetuate
  * an imperial complex — 'we were their rulers'
  * a persecution complex — those who perceive themselves to be thus persecuted, now free, justify their own vendetta against their erstwhile rulers and so the cycle of mutual destruction continues
- In the same vein follows the nostalgia for an imagined history — 'we were so great', 'our boundaries extended a hundred thousand miles in each direction; oh, how have we shrunk'. If the people of a certain nation-religion (the nation and religion confused with each other) ruled over a certain area for a relatively brief period of history, they

continue to claim those areas as parts of their national-religious boundaries and their psyche continues to strive to regain that lost power and glory

- Religion is often used for purely mundane purposes. This is the entire history of Europe, as of many other continents. Examples:
  - looting of the Incas and the Aztecs and building the great cathedrals of Europe
  - preachers exalting the exploited workers to follow the work ethic by not protesting that their twelve-year old children are working sixteen hours a day in the coal mines (as was the case till the end of the 19th century)
  - looting the vanquished so the temple/cathedral/mosque of the conqueror would be enriched
  - priests bound to secular heroes/kings/commanders/presidents doing and saying whatever is expected of them by the donor

Without total personal purification of the priest and the preacher, this trend cannot be stopped and thus the continued misuse of religion for ethnic, national, political and economic purposes cannot cease.

Those who chose the false identity of nation and religion have been the cause of much suffering for humanity. The priests in each country pray for the victory of their countrymen and not for the people of the vanquished lands and nations even though they are of the same religion. In a world where ideals are cherished — in Anglo-French wars, to take a random example, the Anglican priest was as concerned as the loss of the French lives as he grieved over the loss of the English ones, but the

French priest prayed for France, while the English priest prayed for England. And if the French happened to be a Roman Catholic, then, it was understood that they stood no chance to enter heaven so far as the Anglican priest was concerned!

The only way out of this dilemma is to define religion as separate from the nation, state or political groupings. Unfortunately, even in countries where the separation of religion and state is a fundamental principle of the declared polity, the separation has never really occurred because the minds of the people have not changed and pulpits continue to serve as avengers and not redeemers of the sinful 'wicked'.

This is a darker side of the picture of human mind as against the brighter one of which we have listed numerous examples above. It is the strength and purity manifest in these examples that would help divest the religion of all its negative accretions so that religion may serve as only a source of inspiration for non-violence and love.

Those who are pure enough to step out of the false identities imposed upon religion are the reformers and renunciates of history, often persecuted. A careful study of history will show that most often those who have divested themselves of the false identities associated with religion are the contemplatives. They have found their revelations in certain moments of mystery while travelling a path of self-examination, self-purification and thereby a direct experience of God.

It is the contemplatives who have understood that the origin of every religion is in some profound and unique internal experience of divinity that the original founder pursued with great diligence and ascetic endeavour before finding it in the state of such unique and profound consciousness that revelations occurred. It is for this reason that in all continents and among all those people who seek the spiritual truth, they wander off into short or long periods of silence and solitude (Sufi *khalwa*, Sanskrit *ekanta*) that could be only forty days or could be ten years of duration. Once we have found this source of religion in these levels of consciousness, we would not venture to sully the teachings arising out of it; we would try to maintain its purity and, if possible, attempt to replicate the experience, nay, the methodical experiment in the mystic path that the founders of all religions had pursued.

Thus it is the revival of the contemplative and meditative path that will return to us the pure inheritance of the core of spiritual experience and prevent the repeat of the destruction that, as we have said, the false identities imposed on religion. In other words, the unity of religions is to be found in the *dervish*, the *pir*, the mendicant or the wandering *sadhu*. It is they, who from all different religions in the past, often gathered together around some fire outside a wayside inn or a hermit's hut and discoursed about their experience of divinity or shared it in silence. These were the true inter-religious conferences, the effects of which can be seen in the thread of unity and parallel experiences in rituals that we find among all people of the world.

To find unity among all religions we must strive for the unification of the individual soul with the Supreme Consciousness — call it God or name it *Bodhi*. It is to achieve this union with God, which would then unite the spiritual guides of various faiths, that the contemplatives of all traditions went off to dwell in the solitary caves. We read in the ancient *Rig Veda*:

In the cave of the mountains,
at the confluences of the rivers,
one becomes wise by meditation.

Zarathushtra communed with the divine fire in a cave for ten years to receive the revelations bestowed by Ahur Mazda. There is a view that Jesus was not born in the manger but in a cave at Nazareth. The cave of St. Francis of Assisi still invokes a presence of peace in the pilgrim or the occasional visitor. Hazrat Mohammad often withdrew to the cave of Hira where the revelation of the Holy Koran occurred. The great *yogis* still dwell in the Himalyan caves. So do the contemplative Coptic monks who do not leave the underground caves of their monasteries in Ethiopia for many years at a time as also the contemplative monks of Mount Athos in Greece. They all have understood the true origin of religion. Above all, of course, as the *Upanishads* say, is the cave of the heart, which the contemplative has learned to enter for true solitude. This he can do whether he is a cobbler sitting by a city street or a commander in the battlefield.

What do these unifiers of the human soul with God, and consequently the unifiers of humanity, do in the caves of contemplation? Here we repeat some of the parallels among religions which we have listed above. They undertake the practices of silence, fasting, celibacy, prayer, rosary, penitence and changing the position of the mind by experimenting with body positions as well. The disciplines practiced in the periods of solitude cannot always be revealed to the uninitiated lest they cause harm. However, some of these can be undertaken by anyone whether a recluse or a lay woman.

From the vast repertoire of the methodologies of meditation known in the Sino-Indian traditions (*Dhyana-yoga, Jhana,* Ch'an, *Son,* Zen), we take a few that are practiced in common by different religions. The extent of sophistication in the varieties of methods may differ, but many principles of contemplative and meditative practices are held in common by the adherents of different faiths and religions and understanding of these will lead us to the core that cannot fail to unite us, even if we follow different doctrines and various worldviews.

Only when one reaches the pinnacle of the personal experience of the divine does he comprehend the original meaning of the scripture, which records the founder's own inner ecstasy and revelation.

Here are some of the systems of contemplation and meditation that are common to the major religions. They can be listed here only briefly. The detailed practices may take decades to bear fruit, or they may fructify instantly, depending on the practitioner's level of internal purification.

NAMA-SMARANA — REMEMBERING THE DIVINE NAME

Hari hari namu japu prana adharu...
Rama nama japi ekankaru.

— *Guru Granth Sahib*

Different religions and languages have different names for the divinity. The Hindus recite 1,008 names, each as various manifestations of divinity. In Islam there are ninety-nine that are commonly known. There are many ways of remembering the name: singing aloud, reciting, mumbling, thinking the name in the mind and heart which then becomes meditation.

A *guru*, a *pir*, or a spiritual director may assign a particular name for a disciple to recite constantly, with or without a rosary. The higher the spiritual status of the guide, the deeper it is in the mind without vocalisation and greater is the disciple's experience of the name. The disciple approaches the spiritual director with a request to confer to him a divine name for recitation with constant remembrance and promises to oneself to keep it ever in his heart, as we read in the *Guru Granth Sahib*:

Nanaka dijay nama dana
rakhau hiye paroyee.

Thus a divine name may often be used as a *mantra* alone or in combination with other syllables and words. If you have objection to the word *mantra*, call it a one-word prayer in silence. As the meditation grows, the remembrance of the name becomes natural and deeply interiorised.

Such a name, taken into the depths of one's consciousness, releases powerful purificatory energies and generates internal celestial music. The sound of the sacred syllable, the secret of the *mantra* science, brings one face to face with one's beloved God:

Akhara nada kathana bakhiana...
drisatiman akhara hai jeta
nanaka para brahma niralepa.

— *Guru Granth Sahib*

Here it should be remembered that one is advised to hold back the vocalisations. The texts do not say 'repeat the name' but that

Nanaka nama dhiayiye sacchi badiyayi.

— *Guru Granth Sahib*

Says Nanak, meditate on the name and that is true greatness. *Manana* is contemplating on the meaning of a metaphysical phrase, or a word from the scriptures till the meaning becomes a reality to oneself.

In the Christian tradition one may choose, or be given by the

spiritual director, a particular passage from the holy scripture —
a line from a psalm, or a saying of Jesus to read and to ponder
upon; to apply to one's deeper self, to achieve a transformation
within or to experience the closeness to God.

Similarly, the Sufi novitiate is given a phrase from the Holy
Qur'an, the *kalam Allah*, which is 'revealed to humanity wrapped
in many thousands of veils'. The *murid*, disciple, contemplates a
passage assigned by his *pir* till one ceases to be *dar-wujud*, in body,
and has achieved the *nafs-e-haqiqat-e-khud*, the essence of the
reality of self.

Those in the traditions of yoga meditation (belonging to
whichever denomination of religion of Indian origin) are given
similar passages from the Vedic, Buddhist, Jain, Sikh or any other
tradition. The system of contemplation in the traditions of India
is most refined in the Vedanta path. Every novitiate is given a
mahavakya (a great sentence), because of its depth of meaning.
There are four main *mahavakya*s in Vedanta but in other associated
traditions one may choose from over a hundred. For example, the
mahavakya 'Tat tvam asi' (That thou art) may take an entire lifetime
to unravel internally. The *gur-mantar* of the Sikhs, the five
*namakara*s of the Jainas, and so forth – together with additional
passages from the respective scriptures – may be presented to the
mind to contemplate.

In all of these systems, there are parallel methodologies of
using interiorised logic that constitutes *manana* (contemplation),
uha (in the *Yoga-sutras*) and *tarka* in the *tantric* system, the most
essential part of an internal dialogue. Until one has completely
assimilated the innermost meaning of such a word, phrase, or
passage that a self-transformation has been completed, the assigned

passage remains the object of contemplation day and night. So it is among the Sufis, *Vedantins* or *yogis*.

RIDDLES

Mutually contradictory or 'impossible' statements are used by numerous meditative traditions like the passages for contemplation. The purpose is to take the mind beyond common logic, and bring opposite concepts to unification in transcendence. One may be required to unravel the riddle till a spiritual breakthrough and transformation of consciousness occurs. This is again true of all contemplative systems.

BODY POSTURE

Training oneself to assume a certain position for prayer, contemplation and self-conquest is a common method in all religions. The sequence of various body positions in the course of *namaz* or *salat*, is an example of the same.

In Christianity, to pray while sitting on a hard bench, or kneeling, or standing, one becomes so absorbed in prayer and meditation that any bodily discomfort is forgotten. The stories of Christian saints remaining in the same position and praying throughout the night are legendary. The traditions of India, like yoga, are the most sophisticated and detailed in this regard; the Jaina *kayotsarga* practices being the foremost. The Sufi training is not too far behind. The same applies to *mudras*, the hand positions as in Christian or Muslim prayer — the Indian traditions teach hundreds of such positions for different types and stages of prayer and worship.

AMBULATORY PRAYER

Prayer while walking is one of the common practices among the followers of many religions. A Christian, Buddhist or a Hindu monk keeps turning the beads of his rosary or *mala* while walking. It is an inspiring site to see the Turkish people walking the streets of German cities while practising their *tasbeeh*. So also is the Tibetan with his prayer wheel.

One of the common examples of ambulatory prayer is the religious procession or circumambulation of holy sites, sacred cities and edifices, with or without prescribed rituals, practised in all religions. Such ambulatory prayer is an essential part of pilgrimage in all religions.

The deepest practice of the ambulatory prayer is contemplative walking taught in most Buddhist and *swamis'* monasteries, in Sufi *khanqahs*, Zen-dos, and is often practised by Christian monks. One walks to and fro within the confines of parallels lines of suitable length, or in a limited area of the monastery, or within *vyuha* (a pattern), such as a labyrinth. The detailed internal system of the contemplative walk is taught by the masters of various traditions.

CONFESSION

Details of the internal dialogue for self-purification and surrender are the core practices in the contemplative method. One examines one's weaknesses, argues with pros and cons, counters any tendency to 'giving excuses to oneself for oneself', confesses to oneself and renews the vow for self-purification, to free oneself from any *gunah* – sin or *zillat* – a slip. Slowly one fills any remaining gaps between oneself and God. The Christian confesses to his sinfulness; the Hindu recites, *papo-ham*, and seeks to cleanse oneself of the transgressions committed in the day or night in thought, word or deed. In the words of the *Vedas*:

Yad-ahna papam-akarsham...

yad ratrya papam akarsham…

manasa vacha karmana…

So the Mazdayasnian in the liturgies of Khurd-Avesta:

Az an gunah manashni gavashni kunashni,

tani ravani, geti minoani, okhe awakhsh pasheman pa se

gavashni pa patet hom… Kshaothra ahurahe mazda.

Without such recognition of interior impurities one cannot progress to the ideal of evoking the presence of the divine in the earthly.

Such a confession then leads to acts of *prayashchitta* (penitence), not only for transgressions committed but the duties and acts of love, service and devotion omitted:

Kim aham papam akaravam
kim aham sadhu nakaravam
(What transgressions I have committed;
what right acts I have omitted.)

— the Vedic liturgy

In Islam, thus, without *tawba* (repentance), there is no sainthood.

It is in this context of contemplative speaking to one's own mind that we read the many Indian saints' songs addressed to the mind to purify itself, and not to waylay the pilgrim on the path to God:

Karahale mana pardesiya…
mana karahala sati guru purakhu dhiyai…

— *Guru Granth Sahib*

One prays for the removal of all stains and signs of ego and anger from the mind so that the mind may become a fit vehicle to lead one to God:

Jaba ihu mana mahi karata gumana;
taba ihu bavaru phirata bigana.

— *Guru Granth Sahib*

VISUALISATIONS

Many different forms of visualisations with devotion and surrender are practised as part of the contemplative and meditative systems based in the various faiths.

A Christian may visualise the suffering of Christ on the stations of the cross; he may visualise His compassionate visage; or the Pieta figure; or the mental image of a saint. This may be accompanied with the contemplations of sacred phrases as described above.

In the Hindu liturgy, the very first act is the mental recitation of the *dhyana-shloka*, the verse for visualisation meditation, not merely invoking the presence of the divinity but 'seeing' the presence in the mind's eye, full in all iconographic detail.

The most elaborate visualisations are taught in the Tibetan tradition, which we need not depict here. The practice of visualisation as a system of meditation is elaborate and is shared by many traditions. The images repeatedly imprinted upon the mind lead to

- internal transformation
- revelation of the true nature of one's chosen form of the deity
- eventual identification with the divine figure so that the attributes of the divine descend into the very soul of the devotee

One of the forms of visualisation is concentration on the image of a written word or symbol, such as the sign of *Om*, the

Arabic form of *Allah*, a *svastika*, the cross in its many versions, and even the chosen name or *mantra* written and visualised in the usual script. A Sufi may visualise the very first *nuqteh*, *bindu*, the dot under the Arabic letter *bay* (letter 'B') with which the *Qur'an* begins, or one may visualise the same dot on top of the sign for *Om*. Through this literally one-pointed concentration, one may enter the gateway to infinity.

Some visualisations are practised in the heart, some in the forehead, and so forth, together with many possible embellishments. We cannot go into these details in this limited space.

IDENTIFICATION
Whatever one dwells upon, that verily does he becomes:

Yo yach-chraddhah sa eva sah.

When one visualises one's chosen form of divinity, together with the appropriate name, *mantra* or prayer, and becomes a constant baseline thought and a 'feeling' within oneself, the transformation that occurs produces a sense of identity with the Beloved One. Those who thus keep the deity in their heart and mind begin to exhibit traits similar to the object of their worship. The Buddhist develops the Buddha-like mien and *mudra*; the Sufi seeks to become like Ali and Ishmael; the Christian experiences the stigmata. At that point it is difficult to draw the line between the consciousness of the devotee and the deity. When the Vedantic affirmation '*Tat tvam asi*' (That thou art) is applied to *bhakti-yoga* in this relationship, one refers oneself to be 'that', *so-ham* (I am that), *shivo'ham* (I am Shiva), *ana anta wa-anta ana* – says the Sufi (I am you and you are I).

This seeking of some degree of identification to become Christ-like, to become Buddha-like, is common to all religions.

BREATHING

The meditative practice most commonly shared by various religions is that of prayer with breath, which takes many simple or progressively complex forms. Let each breath become a prayer — this is an exhortation to all devotees.

The awareness of breath flow is the primary alphabet of meditation. It is part of the practice of mindfulness (*sati-patthana* in Buddhism, *smrty-upa-sthana* in the *Yoga-sutras*).

In the Vipassana system, no particular prayer word is permitted — that is the general impression. However, the author has met Thai monks who use the name of the Buddha in its Pali language version, *buddho*. In northern Buddhism, as in the yoga tradition, the use of a short *mantra* in synchrony with the breath is a common practice. Similar practices are included in the Jaina meditative tradition of *preksha-dhyana.*

One learns to breathe diaphragmatically — breathe slowly, gently, without a jerk, and without a sound in the breath; feel the flow and touch of the breath in the nostrils. One keeps the *mantra* or the prayer word flowing in the mind while sensing and observing the gentle breath-flow.

This practice has many variations, which are prescribed by the meditation guide to students of different capacities and personalities. For example, observing the breath-flow from the navel and letting the word also to flow, or remembering the word in the cavity of the heart.

The Buddhist and yoga meditation practices of breath meditation have exact identical parallels in the Sufi practice of *dhikr* (*zikr*). So also the Christian meditative tradition, like the hesychasm which includes the exactly same methods. Even

St. Ignatius of Loyola includes prayer with breath rhythms in his *Spiritual Exercises*.

We read in the Sikh scripture:

Sasi sasi aradhe niramala soi janu.

— *Guru Granth Sahib*

Only one who worships in every breath becomes a pure person. The practices of prayer and meditation with breath awareness are the most commonly shared ones among various religions.

COMMON PRAYER

In inter-religious gatherings it has been a common practice for the guides of different faiths to lead a prayer, each according to his tradition. The true unity of prayer, however, occurs in silence. Even though it is customary to take a minute or two of silence to mark special events, the true meditative and contemplative silence of the mind is rare.

Only the minds at peace within can deliberate on ways of finding peace among societies. The minds that are not harmonised within cannot bring about harmony in the external world of relationships. It would be best that wherever people of different faiths, languages, nationalities gather together, they begin and end their deliberations by entering a deep state of silence through the practice of prayer in each breath. Its efficacy for bringing a sense of unity and a feeling of peace can be demonstrated universally in not more than five minutes of silence, guided by one who is proficient in meditation.

An objection may be raised to this 'method in silence' by those who do not believe in any form of prayer. Even then, meditation practice without a prayer or a sacred phrase can be proved to affect a peaceful state of mind. This has been proved in numerous medical and scientific experiments. It is indeed possible to meditate without having a belief in God or prayer. Follow the same method of breath awareness as described above and simply count the breaths. Again, there are many ways to do the count in various permutations, which can be learnt from an authentic teacher.

Here we need to address one more question — in the inter-religious gatherings, how many religions are truly represented? The economically disadvantaged and not very articulate in the modern terminologies have no influence on the deliberations and decision-making processes. Only the 'great religions of the world' have a voice. What distinguishes the 'great religions' from the 'not so great' ones? Is it the economic or political power? Is it contemporary influence through that power? What does that have to do with true spirituality? Is it the large number of adherents? Who are we to say that the fact of an idea that is upheld by a large number constitutes its greatness as an idea *per se*?

Are we great because we are aggressive conquerors who have decimated the numbers, power and strength of the weaker vanquished ones and used that power-mongering as an argument in favour of our greatness whereas in the eyes of God, as we know, it is the meek who are truly great.

Considering the way we weigh and view the greatness of a religion, would Shinto be included among the 'great religions' if Japan, perchance, had won the war? Would *voodoo* be a 'great religion' if its adherents had not been colonised, enslaved and developed economic power?

In the view of a silent meditator, a religion is great not on these grounds but because

- it has influenced the past history in a selfless and beneficial way and has given birth and impetus to arts, sciences and peaceful social structures
- its ideas are philosophically sound and lead to spiritual elevation of the human mind

Thus, the Zarathushtrian tradition with maximum quarter million adherents, the Jaina faith with a few million followers, as well as some of the indigenous traditions worldwide are just as great as the more populous religions that hold the reins of secular power and use it to prove that they are thereby great. In our endeavours for unity among religions we need to undertake *inter alia* the following measures:

- The adherents of different faiths resolve not to judge the value of a religion as great or small but include all religions in their deliberations regarding whatever affects the humanity at large
- The leaders, guides and scholars of each religion institute research into their own past and confess to themselves and then to the world regarding their own historical transgressions against the peoples of other faiths — did we destroy the places of worship of any other religion; did we use force or fraud, and so forth? Then they apologise and atone for the transgressions committed
- Resolve not to condemn the adherents of other religions nor criticise or denounce their doctrine, belief system and practices. Rather, state only our own belief systems, recognising the beauty of those of others with reverence and in a spirit of love
- Undertake research into

* the commonalities of religious belief and spiritual experience
* the examples of mutual respect and accommodation in the vast areas of history so as to learn from the same the answers to the problems of our contemporary strife

• Prepare textbooks showing the commonalities of religious experiences while *respectfully* recognising the beauty of particular beliefs that are specific to certain religions

• As a part of peace education, undertake to train the minds to be at peace through the practice of meditation by making para-religious meditation practice as a highly recommended part of the curriculum in schools worldwide. For the non-believers also the completely religion-neutral meditation systems are suggested

• Honour the wise and the elders of all religions equally

May human beings learn to remember what has been harmonious and beautiful in the past and may they recognise what is right in the present.

PART SIX

THE POETRY OF YOGA

CHAPTER 1

WHAT IS YOGA?

Yoga is to weigh the universe with a feather-light breath.

Yoga is the silence of the soul now being conceived.

Yoga is a Bodhi tree.

Yoga is Siddhartha sitting forty-nine days and nights absolutely still.

Yoga is the forest clearing where the *Upanishad* recites itself.

Yoga is the sacred fire whose flames are the Vedic chants.

Yoga is the cave wherein Zarathushtra holds discourses with fire for ten years in silence.

Yoga is the burning bush whereby Moses is initiated into the secret name, 'I am'.

Yoga is the yoke of the chariot whereon Krishna sits to show to Arjuna the universe-body of self.

Yoga is the revelation of the cosmos-epic in a micro-moment's lightning which is thereupon recited in a million aeons.

Yoga is the crystal of intuition in which no colour, but light alone, reflects.

Yoga is a wordless song, depth that is height, a breath that breathes most only when it ceases.

Yoga is the meekest power, weaponless warrior, motion as stillness, the feast of fasting, soundless shout, the river of resilience, thoughtless thought, and the mind abandoned and left behind.

Yoga is the Mother Grace, the infinity face to face where rocks turn into fathomless, boundless space.

Any less, then it is mere yoga. Yoga is that which grants one the 'nothing'.

A yoga centre is one where aspirants sit not within four walls but have their meditation seats inside the *guru's* vastly expanded heart cave.

May your self be granted such a yoga centre where under your meditation shawl a million souls receive a motherly asylum into soothing solitude and a healing by silence.

May the yoga centre be found contained within this point.

CHAPTER 2

YOGA IS THE MESSAGE

Yoga is the whispering voice within us that calls us to listen, but not to speak.

Yoga is the mind of saints and masters that has made our own mind its home.

Yoga is the wandering mendicant singing his ecstasy of solitude.

Yoga is the mystery that unveils all mysteries so that the meaning of 'no' may be read in the heart *sutra* and the meaning of 'yes' may be understood from the *Upanishads*.

Yoga is the dance of light in the cosmic hall where 'yes' is the meaning of 'no', and 'no' dwells as all consciousness beyond consciousness.

Yoga is *pranayama* that begins when breath is left behind.

Yoga is knowledge that commences where the words are abandoned.

Yoga, *samadhi*, is the nature of all mind whereby the mind may leave itself behind.

Yoga is non-anger; yoga is non-competitiveness; yoga is

uncomplaining; yoga is bending down before those who stand tall.

Yoga is to reach out to those with whom we have disagreed.

Yoga is to apologise for the mistakes we think we have not made.

Yoga is to inaugurate a centre of consciousness in us daily.

Yoga is to consecrate a temple in our hearts nightly.

Beyond wakefulness, dream and sleep, beyond the meditation ladder's last rung is yoga.

I pray that you make yourself small,

that you make amends before you announce yourself,

that you declare yourself as the smallest of teachers and all others be greater than you,

that you surrender the word 'mine' and remember the word 'thine'

so that a temple of the heart may be inaugurated in your city – and whoever enters this temple immediately enters the state of calm.

May you not seek the company of those who rule and govern; may they seek you to learn that self-governance is the true governance.

May you give priority to others who lead their students in yoga and yourself be the last.

May you bow to all and avoid those who wish to bow to you.

May you never become famous or powerful but may the famous and the powerful come to your doorsteps to forget their fame and power, to be made as small as your own being, in humility and in lovingness.

I congratulate you on such an inauguration. I wish you neither success nor absence of success, but the presence of the masters, wherever you sit and enter your own stillness.

May you never know when you have been made great by following this counsel from the tradition of the *yogis*.

May your students prosper in the wealth that makes no claim to being wealth. May they be enriched through the riches that renunciation alone confers.

Swami Veda Bharati

Swami Veda Bharati